COME FLY AWAY

JAMES L. NEDERLANDER   NICHOLAS HOWEY   W.A.T., LTD.
TERRY ALLEN KRAMER   PATRICK CATULLO/JON B. PLATT   JERRY FRANKEL   RONALD FRANKEL/MARC FRANKEL   ROY FURMAN
ALLAN S. GORDON/ELAN MCALLISTER   JAM THEATRICALS   STEWART F. LANE/BONNIE COMLEY   MARGO LION/DARYL ROTH
HAL LUFTIG/YASUHIRO KAWANA   PITTSBURGH CLO/GSFD   SPARK PRODUCTIONS   THE WEINSTEIN COMPANY   BARRY AND FRAN WEISSLER

Present

Concept and Book by
TWYLA THARP

Vocals by
FRANK SINATRA

COME FLY AWAY
A NEW MUSICAL

BY SPECIAL ARRANGEMENT WITH THE FRANK SINATRA FAMILY AND FRANK SINATRA ENTERPRISES

Starring
MATTHEW STOCKWELL DIBBLE   HOLLEY FARMER   LAURA MEAD   CHARLIE NESHYBA-HODGES
RIKA OKAMOTO   KARINE PLANTADIT   KEITH ROBERTS   JOHN SELYA

With
ALEXANDER BRADY   TODD BURNSED   CAROLYN DOHERTY   HEATHER HAMILTON
MEREDITH MILES   ERIC MICHAEL OTTO   JUSTIN PECK

KRISTINE BENDUL   COLIN BRADBURY   JEREMY COX   AMANDA EDGE   CODY GREEN
LAURIE KANYOK   MARIELYS MOLINA   JOEL PROUTY   RON TODOROWSKI   ASHLEY TUTTLE

and
Featured Vocalists
HILARY GARDNER   ROSENA M. HILL

Scenic Design
JAMES YOUMANS

Costume Design
KATHERINE ROTH

Lighting Design
DONALD HOLDER

Sound Design
PETER MCBOYLE

Additional Orchestrations & Arrangements by
DON SEBESKY
DAVE PIERCE

Original Music Supervisor
SAM LUTFIYYA

Music Supervisor & Music Coordinator
PATRICK VACCARIELLO

Conductor/Pianist
RUSS KASSOFF

Casting
STUART HOWARD,
AMY SCHECTER, PAUL HARDT

Press Representatives
THE HARTMAN GROUP
ELLEN JACOBS ASSOCIATES

Marketing
SCOTT A. MOORE

Creative Consultant
CHARLES PIGNONE

Production Executive
RANDALL A. BUCK

Resident Director
KIM CRAVEN

Production Stage Manager
RICK STEIGER

Technical Supervisor
DAVID BENKEN

General Management
THE CHARLOTTE WILCOX COMPANY

Conceived, Choreographed and Directed by
TWYLA THARP

World Premiere at Alliance Theatre, Atlanta, GA
Susan V. Booth, Artistic Director   Thomas Pechar, Managing Director

ISBN 978-1-4234-9383-9

HAL•LEONARD
CORPORATION
7777 W. BLUEMOUND RD. P.O. BOX 13819 MILWAUKEE, WI 53213

D0584760

For all works contained herein:
Unauthorized copying, arranging, adapting, recording, Internet posting, public performance,
or other distribution of the printed music in this publication is an infringement of copyright.
Infringers are liable under the law.

Visit Hal Leonard Online at
www.halleonard.com

BODY AND SOUL

Words by EDWARD HEYMAN,
ROBERT SOUR and FRANK EYTON
Music by JOHN GREEN

Copyright © 1930 Warner Bros. Inc.
Copyright renewed; extended term of Copyright deriving from Edward Heyman assigned and effective January 1, 1987 to Range Road Music Inc. and Bug Music-Quartet Music
Extended term of Copyright deriving from John Green, Robert Sour and Frank Eyton assigned to Warner Bros. Inc. and Druropetal Music
This arrangement Copyright (c) 1993 Range Road Music Inc., Bug Music-Quartet Music, Warner Bros. Inc. and Druropetal Music
International Copyright Secured   All Rights Reserved
Used by Permission

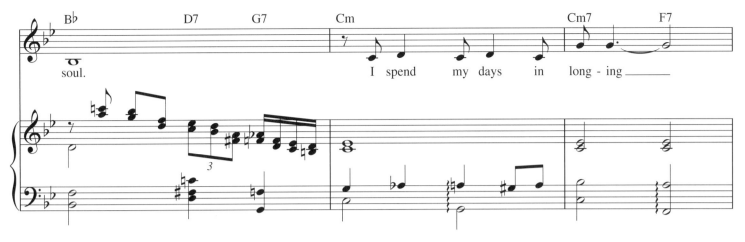

I spend my days in long - ing

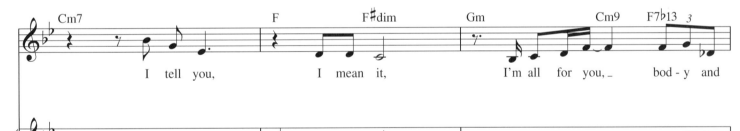

and wond-'ring why _____ it's me you're wrong - ing.

I tell you, I mean it, I'm all for you, _ bod - y and

soul. I can't be-lieve it; it's

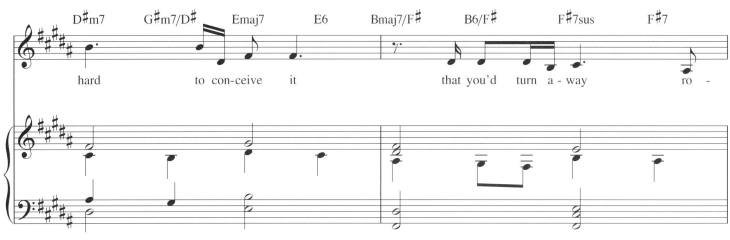

hard to con-ceive it that you'd turn a-way ro -

mance. Are you pre-tend - ing?

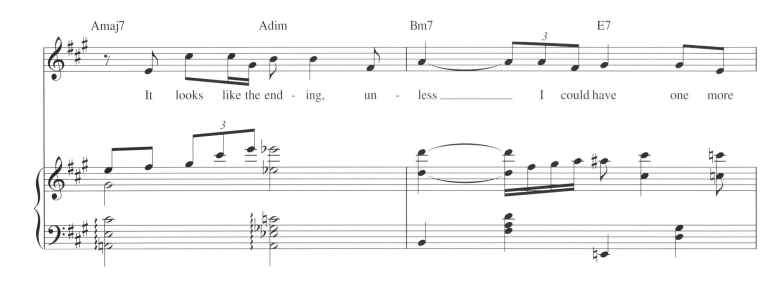

It looks like the end - ing, un - less _____ I could have one more

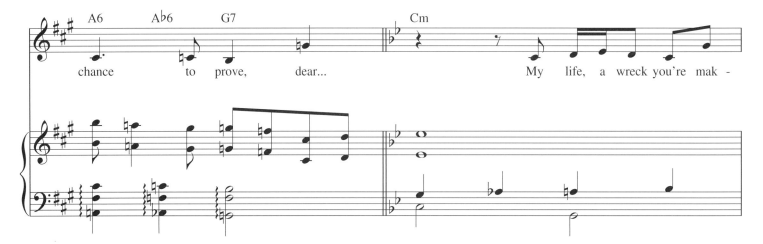

chance to prove, dear... My life, a wreck you're mak -

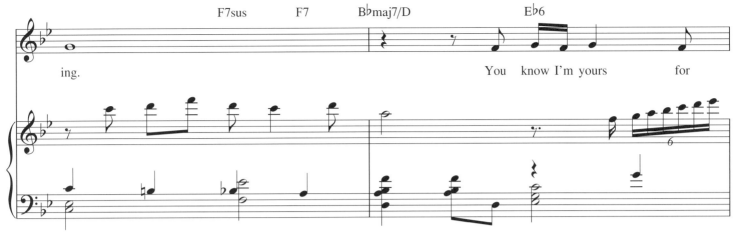

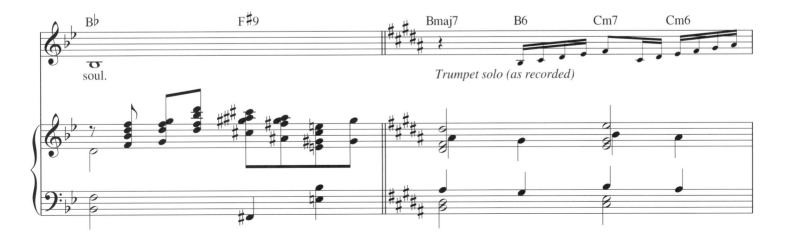

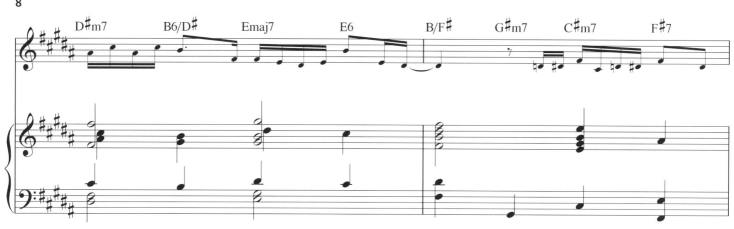

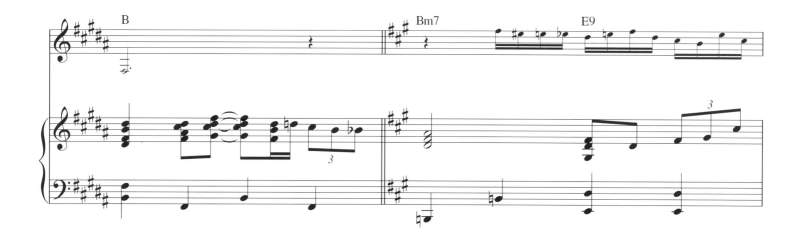

(Solo ends) My life a wreck you're

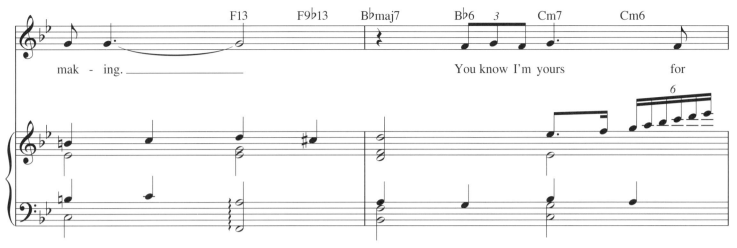

mak - ing. _____ You know I'm yours for

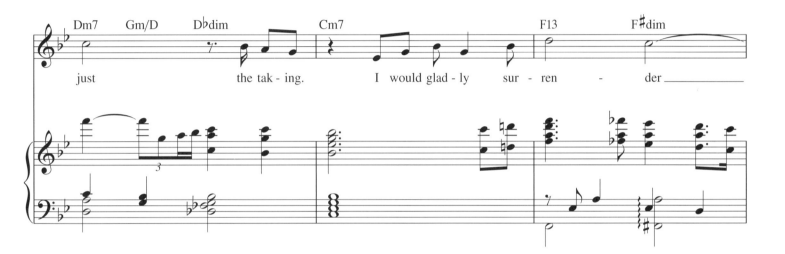

just the tak - ing. I would glad - ly sur - ren - der _____

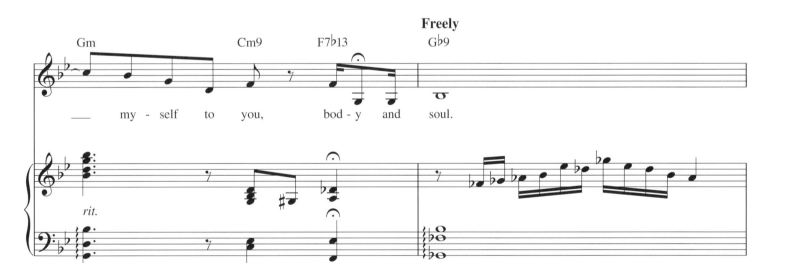

Freely

_____ my - self to you, bod - y and soul.

COME FLY WITH ME

Words by SAMMY CAHN
Music by JAMES VAN HEUSEN

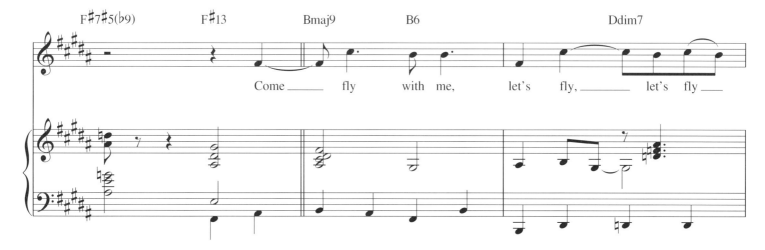

Come ___ fly with me, let's fly, ___ let's fly ___

a - way. ___ If you ___ can use ___ some

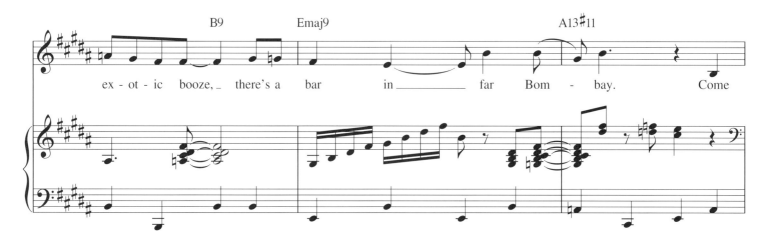

ex - ot - ic booze, _ there's a bar in ___ far Bom - bay. Come

Copyright © 1958 Cahn Music Co., WB Music Corp. and Maraville Music Corp.
Copyright Renewed
All Rights for Cahn Music Co. Administered by WB Music Corp.
International Copyright Secured   All Rights Reserved

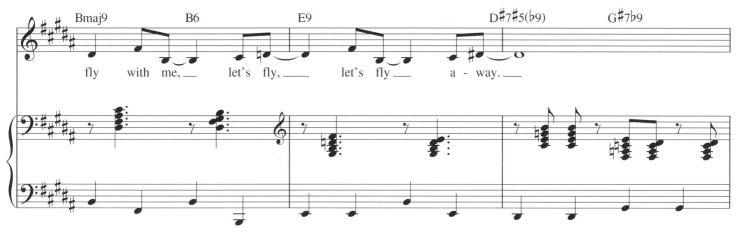

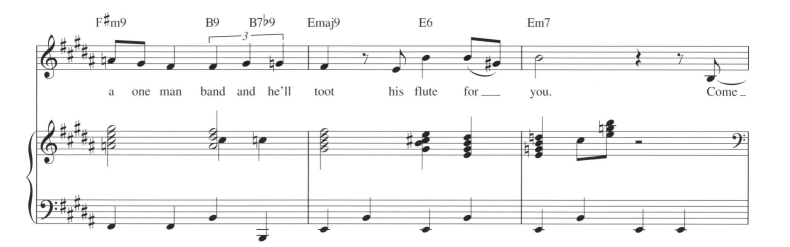

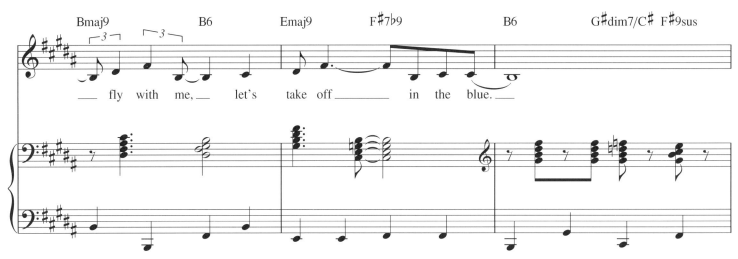

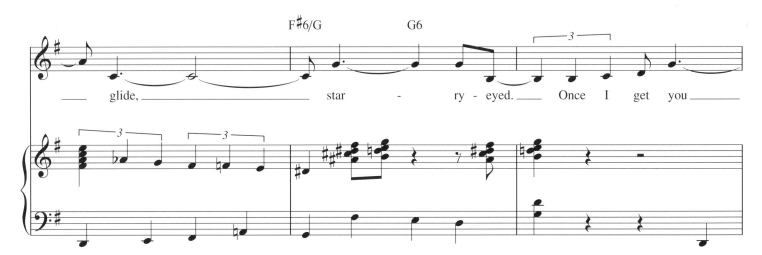

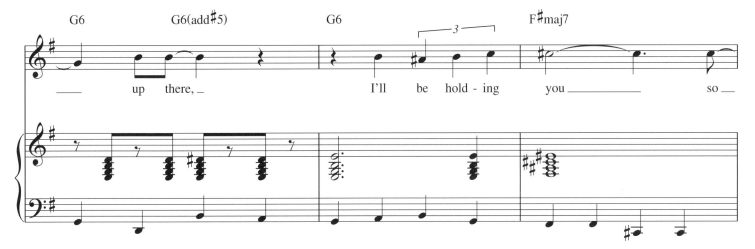

up there, ___ I'll be hold - ing you ___ so ___

___ near you ___ may hear an -

- gels cheer, 'cause ___ we're to - geth - er.

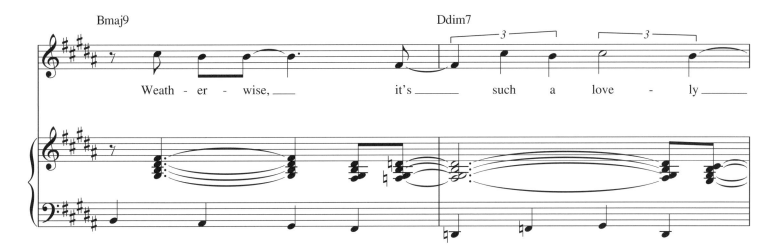

Weath - er - wise, ___ it's ___ such a love - ly ___

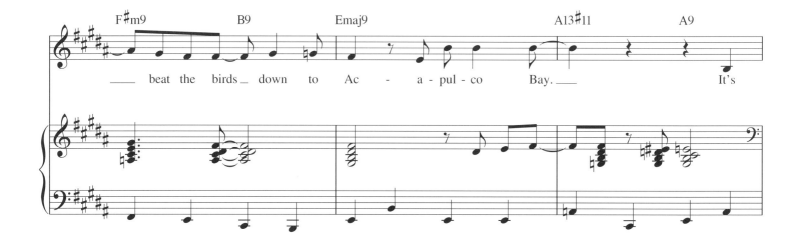

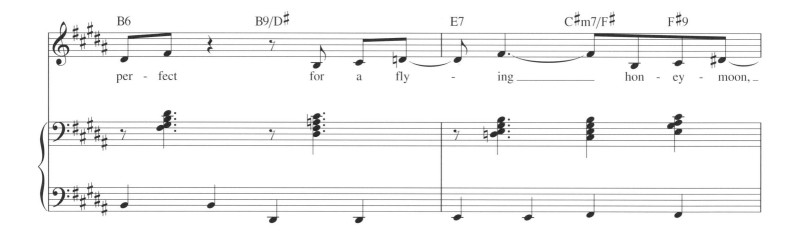

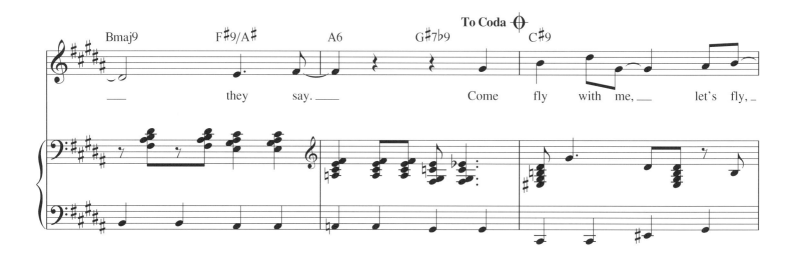

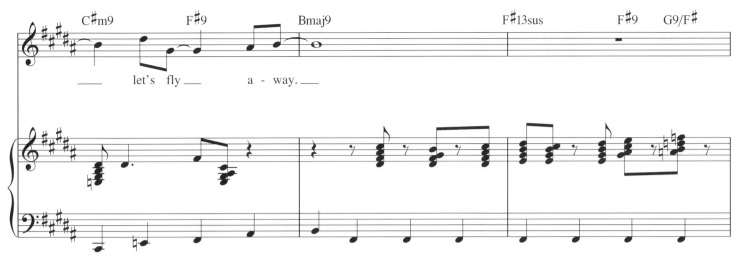

let's fly ___ a - way. ___

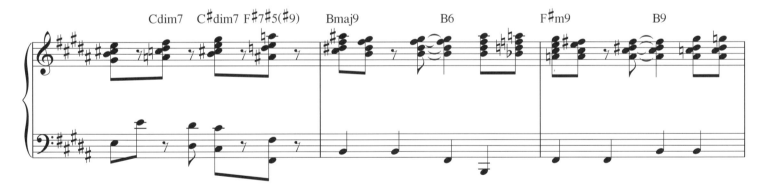

Once I get you ___

CODA

fly with me, ___ let's fly, ___ let's fly. ___

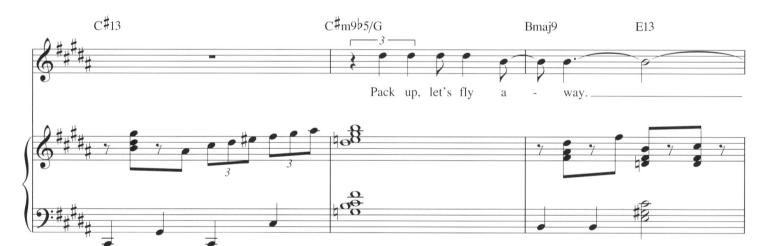

Pack up, let's fly a - way. ___

FLY ME TO THE MOON
(In Other Words)

Words and Music by
BART HOWARD

TRO - © Copyright 1954 (Renewed) Hampshire House Publishing Corp., New York, NY
International Copyright Secured
All Rights Reserved Including Public Performance For Profit
Used by Permission

Em7　　　A7　　　　Dm7　　　　　　　　　　　　　　　　　　　　G7　Cmaj7　　　C/G　C6

In oth-er words, _　ba - by, kiss _ me.

Bm7♭5　　　E7♭9　　　Am7　　　　　　　Dm7　　　　　　　　G7

Fill my heart with song _ and let me sing _ for - ev - er - more. _

Cmaj7　　　C7　　　　F6　　　　　　　Bm7♭5　　　　E7

You _ are _ all I long _ for, all I wor-ship and a - dore. _

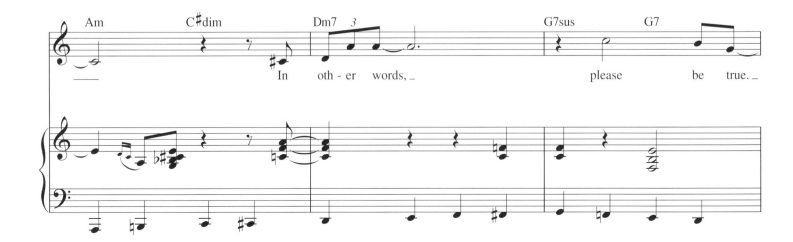

Am　　　　C#dim　　　Dm7　　　　　　　　　　　G7sus　　　G7

In oth - er words, _　please be true. _

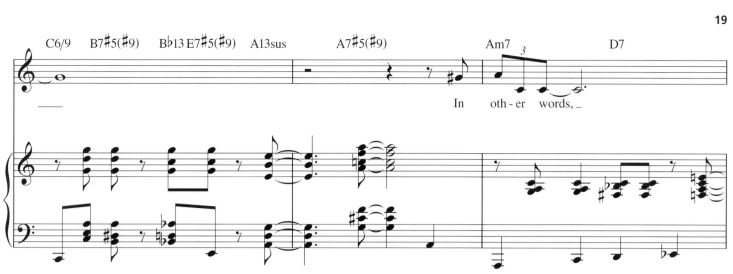

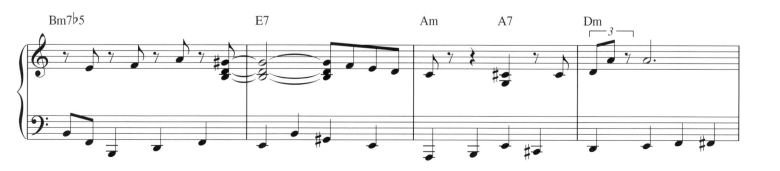

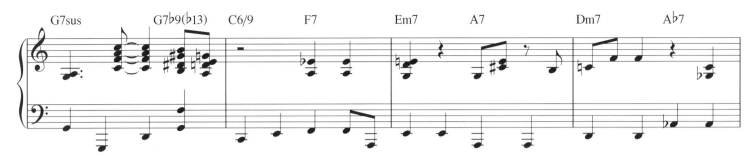

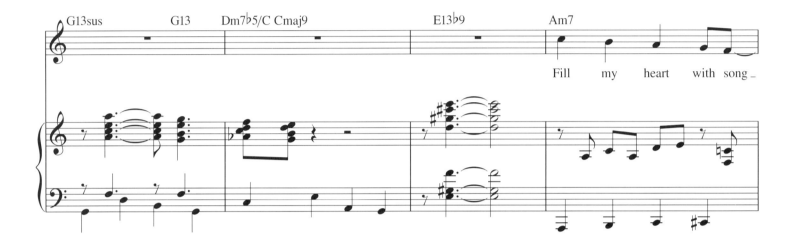

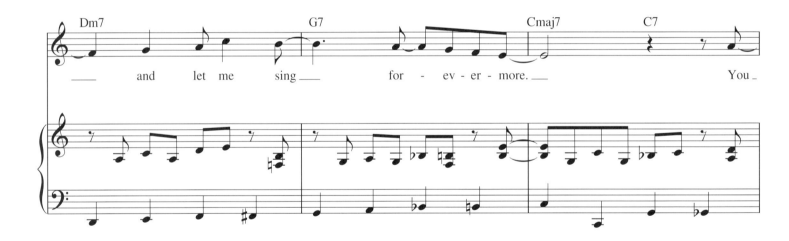

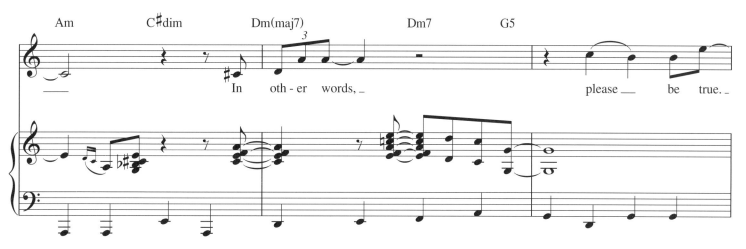

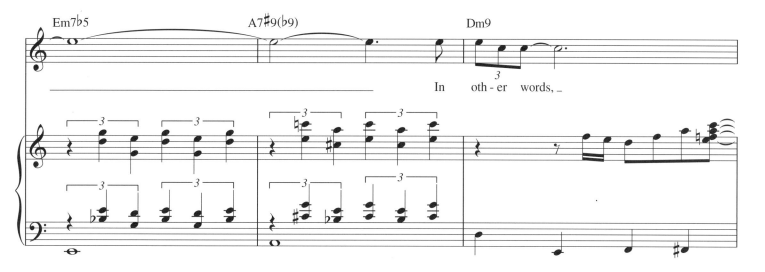

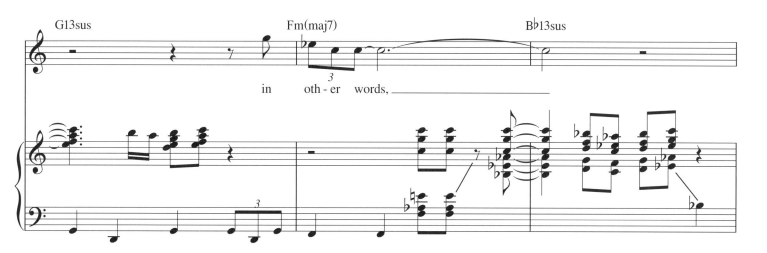

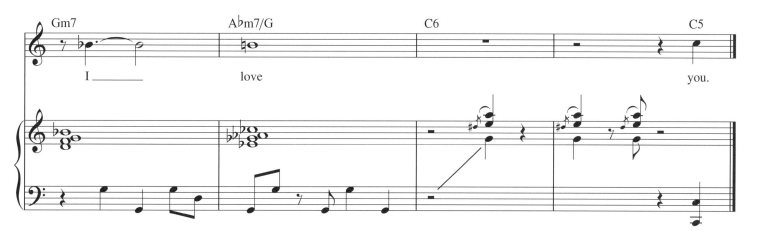

I'VE GOT A CRUSH ON YOU

Music and Lyrics by GEORGE GERSHWIN
and IRA GERSHWIN

Slowly, freely in 2

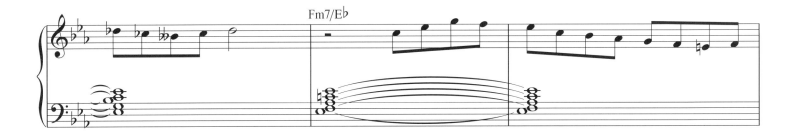

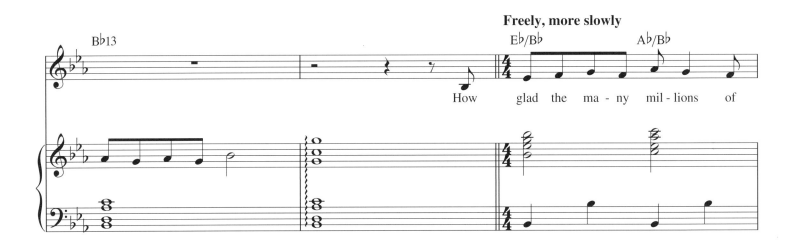

Freely, more slowly

How glad the ma-ny mil-lions of

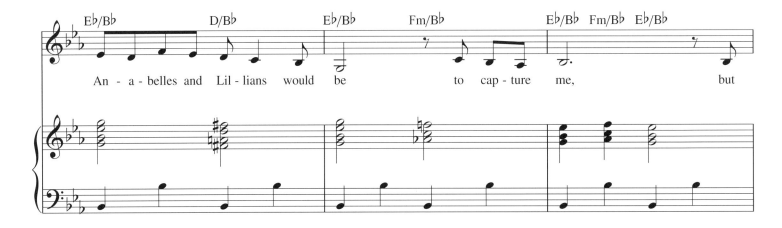

An - a - belles and Lil - lians would be to cap - ture me, but

© 1930 (Renewed) WB MUSIC CORP.
All Rights Reserved   Used by Permission

you had such per-sis-tance you wore down my re-sis-tance. I fell, and it was

swell. I'm your big and brave and hand-some Ro-me-o. How I won you, I shall nev-er, nev-er know. It's

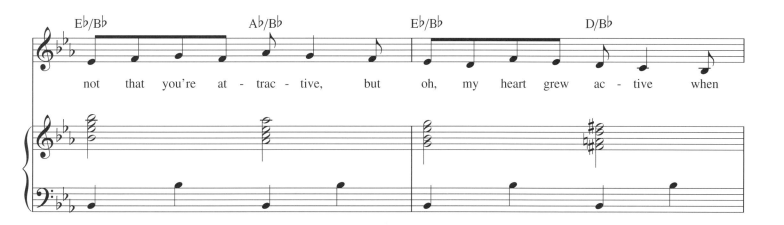

not that you're at-trac-tive, but oh, my heart grew ac-tive when

could you care ___ for a cun-ning cot-tage

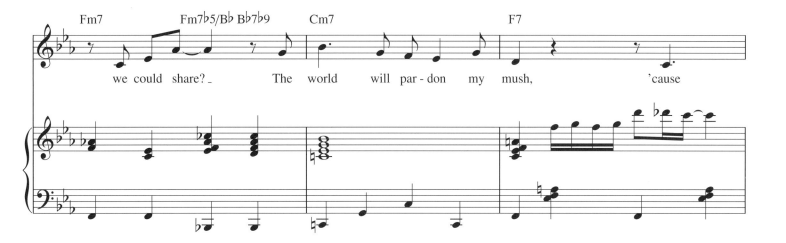

we could share? _ The world will par-don my mush, 'cause

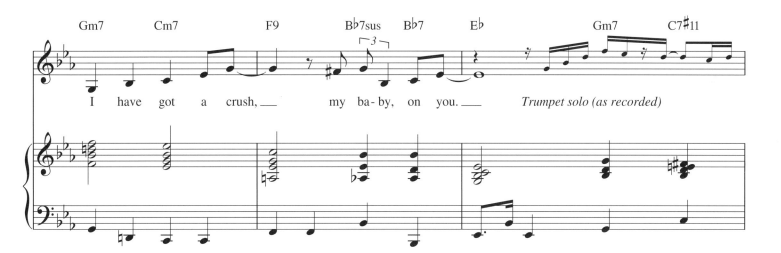

I have got a crush, ___ my ba-by, on you. ___ *Trumpet solo (as recorded)*

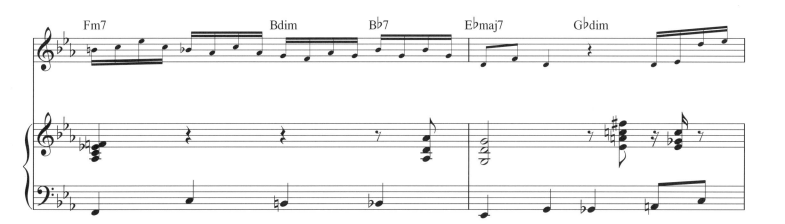

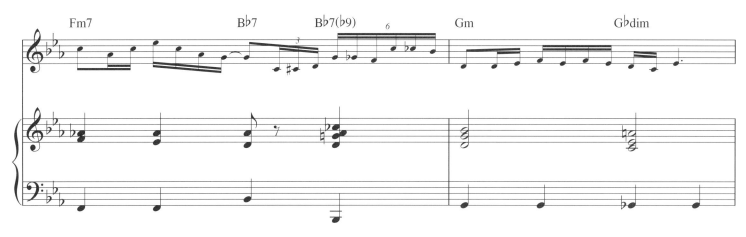

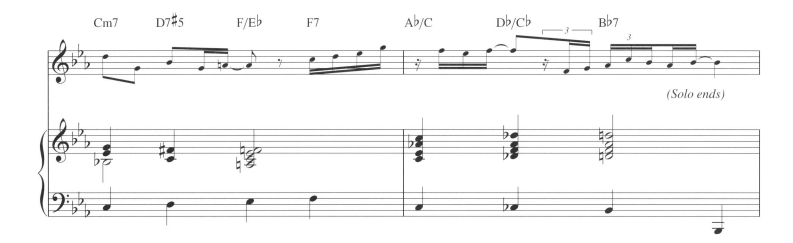

(Solo ends)

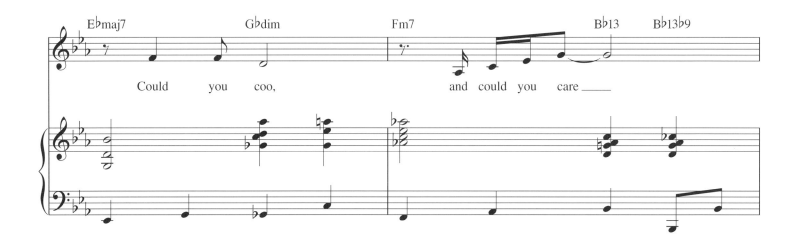

Could you coo, and could you care ____

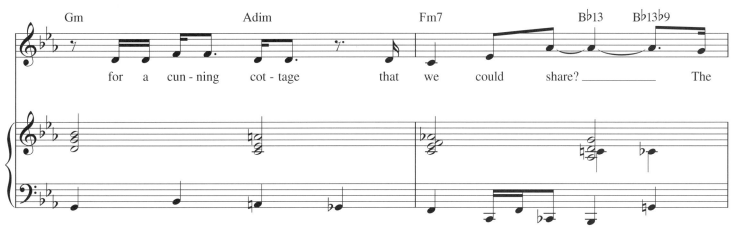

for a cun - ning cot - tage that we could share? _____ The

world will par - don my mush, 'cause ___ I have got a

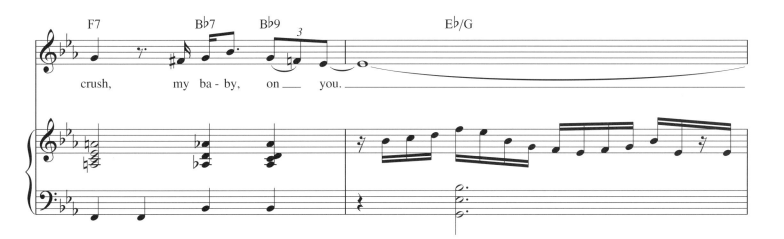

crush, my ba - by, on ___ you. _____

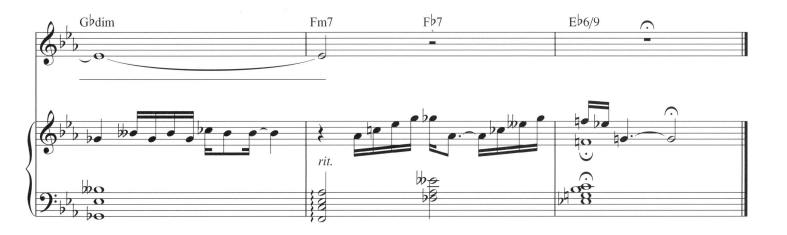

I'VE GOT THE WORLD ON A STRING

Lyric by TED KOEHLER
Music by HAROLD ARLEN

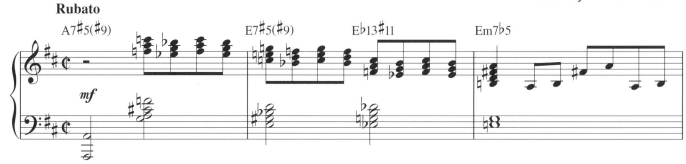

I've got the world ___ on a string. ___ Sit-tin' on a

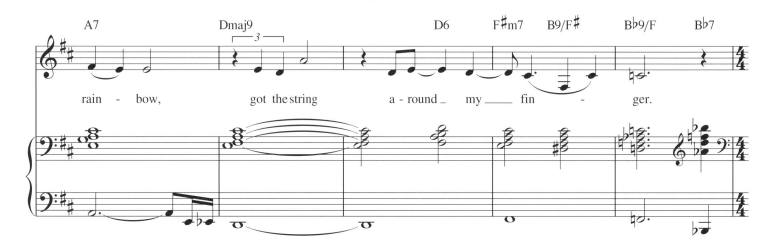

rain - bow, got the string a - round _ my ___ fin - ger.

What a world, _____ what a life, _ I'm in love.

© 1932 (Renewed 1960) TED KOEHLER MUSIC CO. (ASCAP)/Administered by BUG MUSIC and S.A. MUSIC CO.
All Rights Reserved   Used by Permission

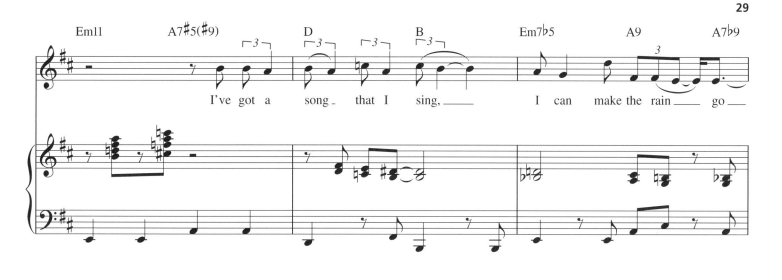

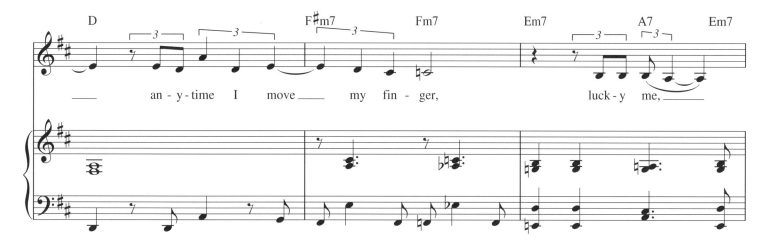

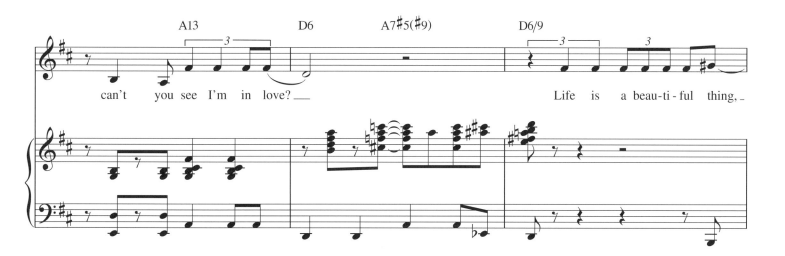

I'd be a sil-ly so and ____ so ____ if I should ev-er let it go. ____

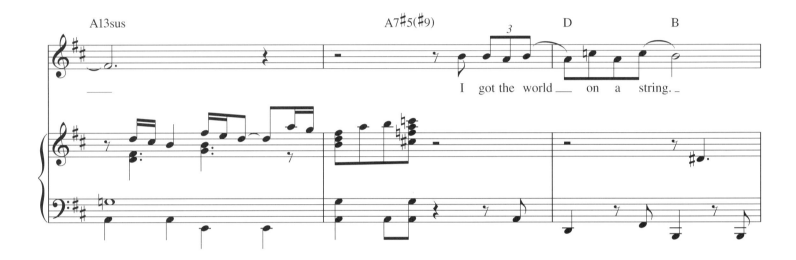

____ I got the world ____ on a string. ____

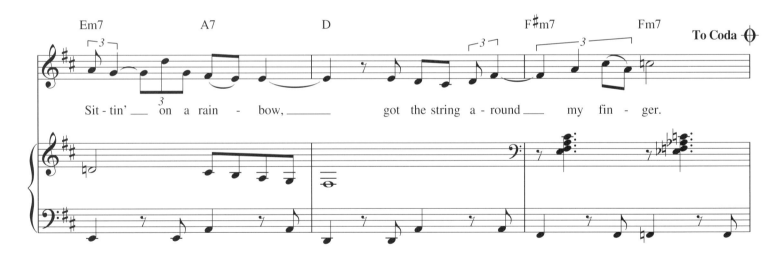

Sit-tin' ____ on a rain - bow, ____ got the string a-round ____ my fin - ger.

What a world, ____ what a life, ____ I'm in love. ____

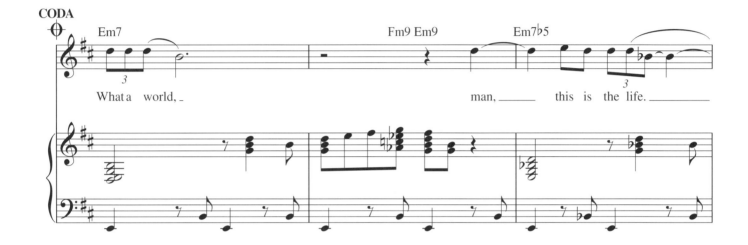

I'VE GOT YOU UNDER MY SKIN

Words and Music by
COLE PORTER

Moderate Swing

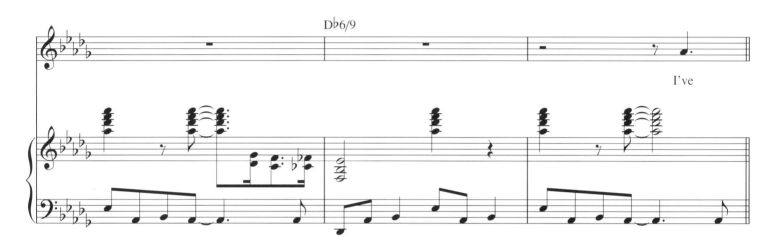

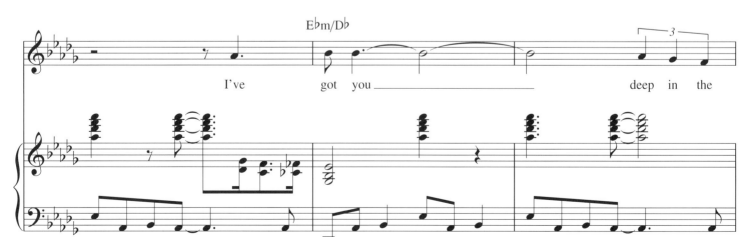

Copyright © 1936 by Chappell & Co.
Copyright Renewed, Assigned to Robert H. Montgomery, Trustee of the Cole Porter Musical and Literary Property Trusts
Chappell & Co. owner of publication and allied rights throughout the world
International Copyright Secured   All Rights Reserved

heart of __ me, _____ so deep __ in my heart __

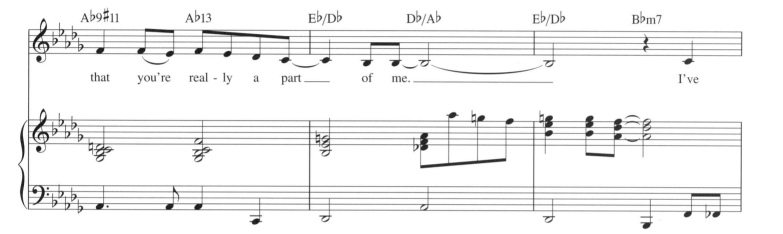

that you're real-ly a part ___ of me. _____ I've

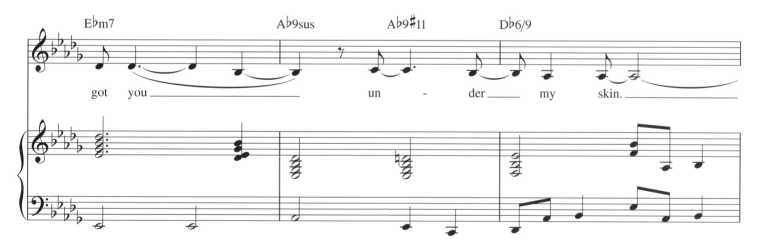

got you _____ un - der ___ my skin. _____

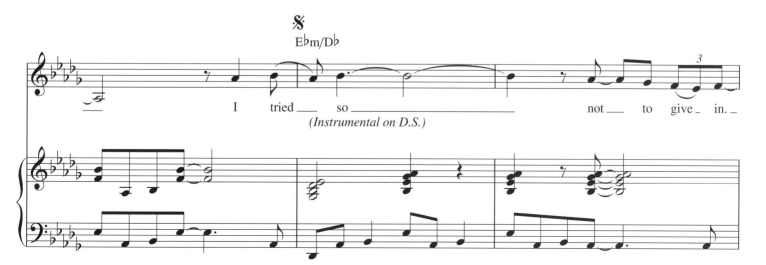

I tried __ so _____ not __ to give _ in.

(Instrumental on D.S.)

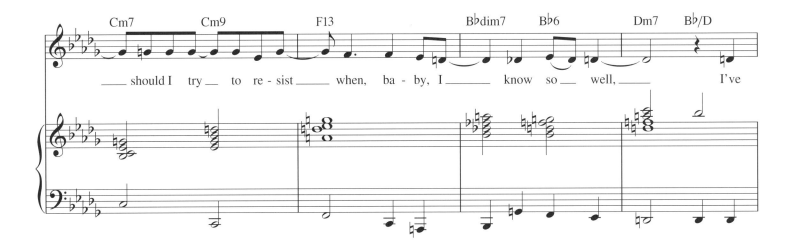

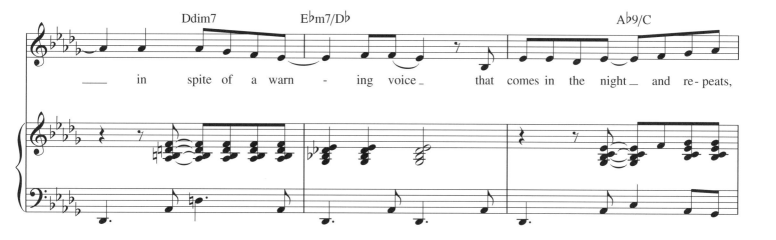

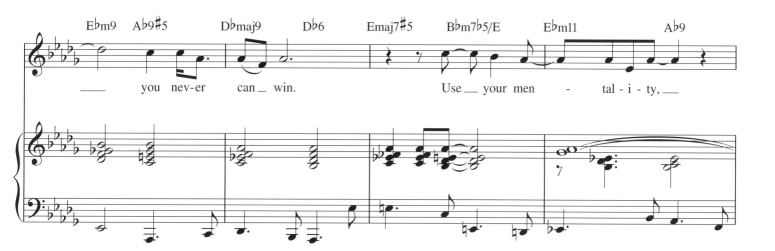

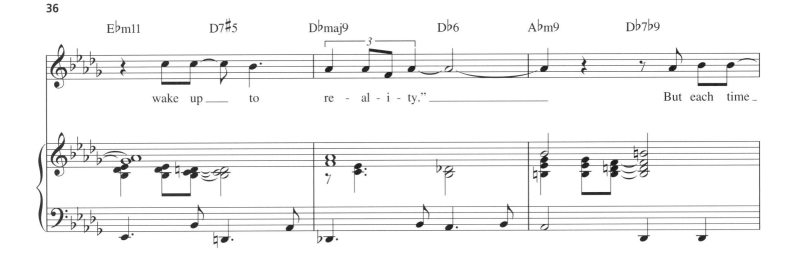

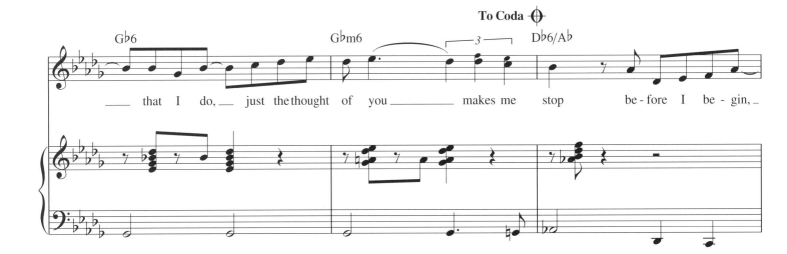

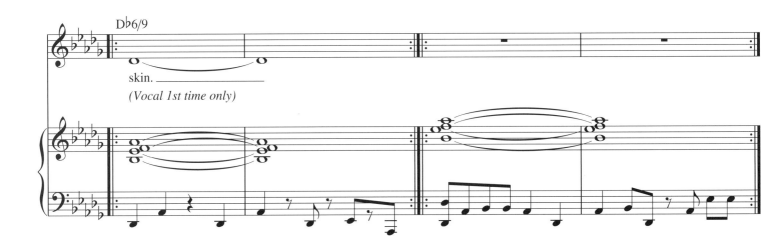

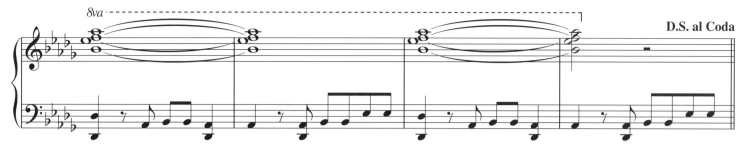

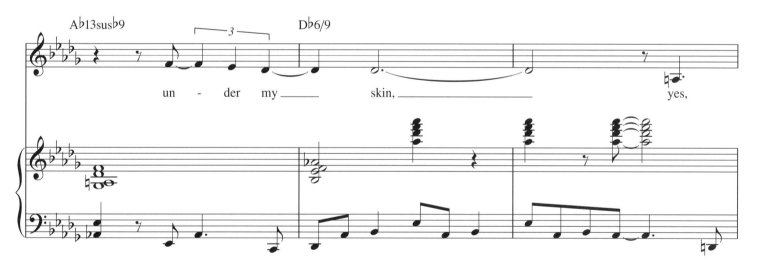

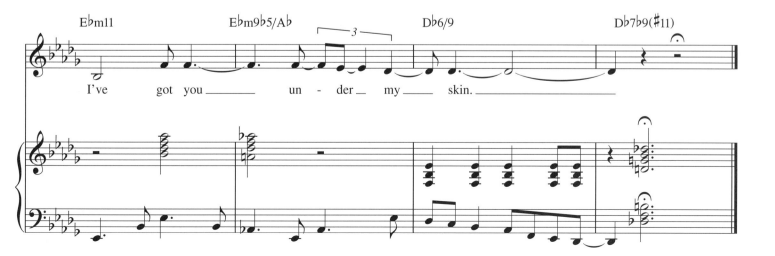

IT'S ALL RIGHT WITH ME

Words and Music by
COLE PORTER

Copyright © 1953 by Cole Porter
Copyright Renewed, Assigned to Robert H. Montgomery, Trustee of the Cole Porter Musical and Literary Property Trusts
Chappell & Co. owner of publication and allied rights throughout the world
International Copyright Secured   All Rights Reserved

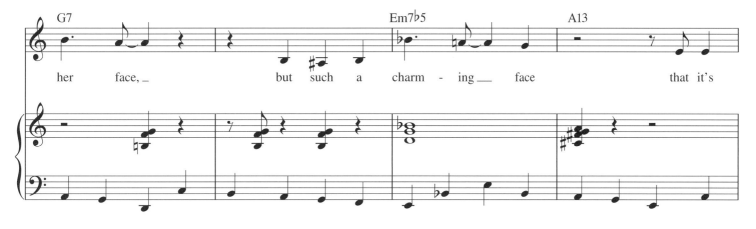

her face, _ but such a charm - ing _ face that it's

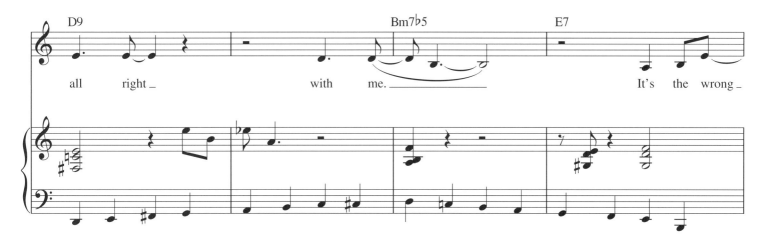

all right _ with me. _____ It's the wrong _

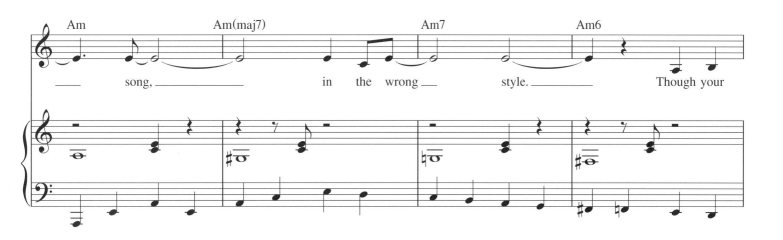

_ song, _____ in the wrong _ style. _____ Though your

smile is _ love - ly, it's the wrong _ smile. It's not

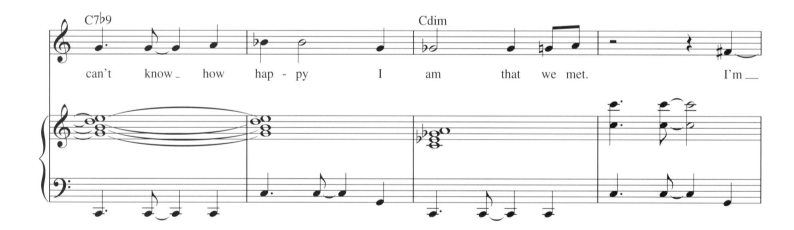

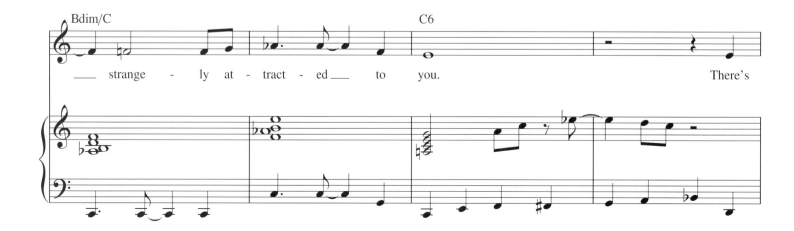

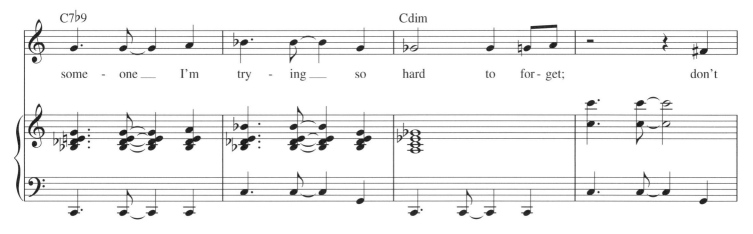

some-one ___ I'm try-ing ___ so hard to for-get; don't

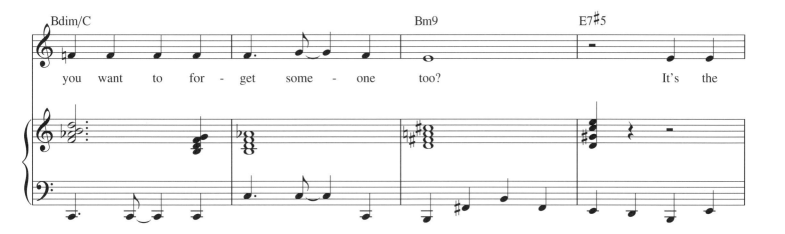

you want to for-get some-one too? It's the

wrong game, _____ with the wrong ___ chips. Though your

lips are ___ tempt-ing, they're the wrong ___ lips. They're not

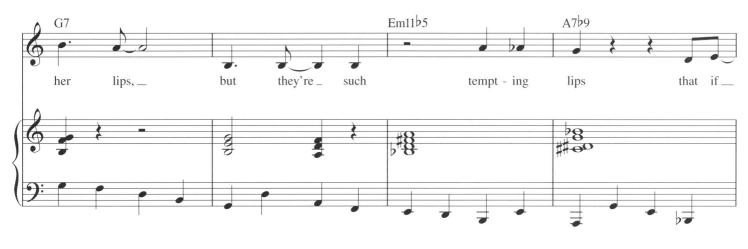

her lips, _ but they're _ such tempt - ing lips that if _

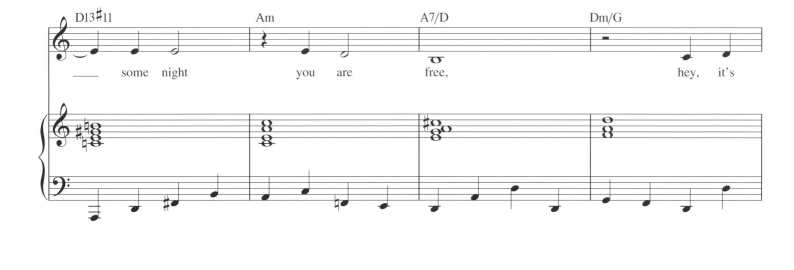

_ some night you are free, hey, it's

all right, _ it's all right, _ it's

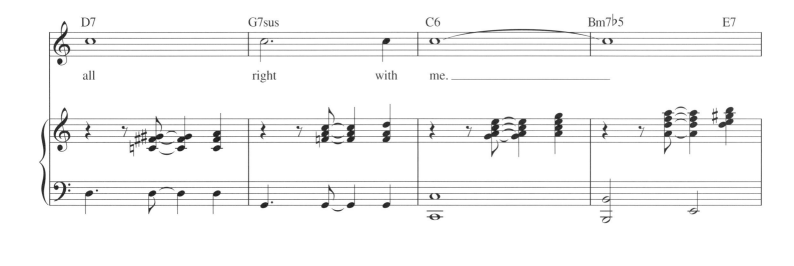

all right with me. ___

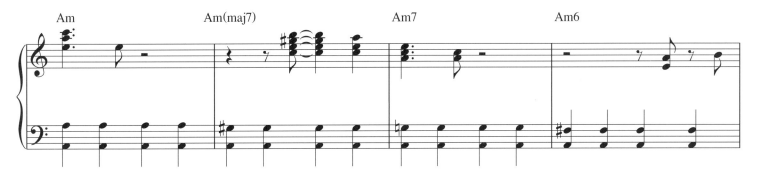

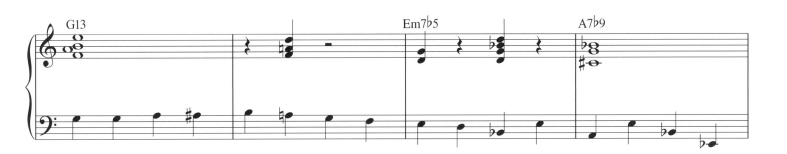

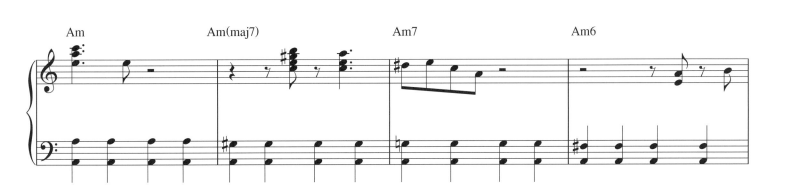

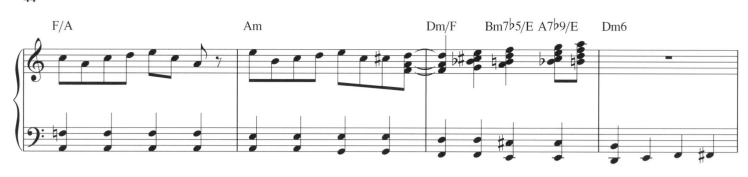

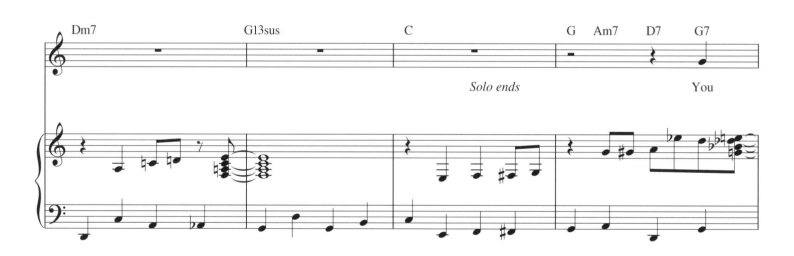

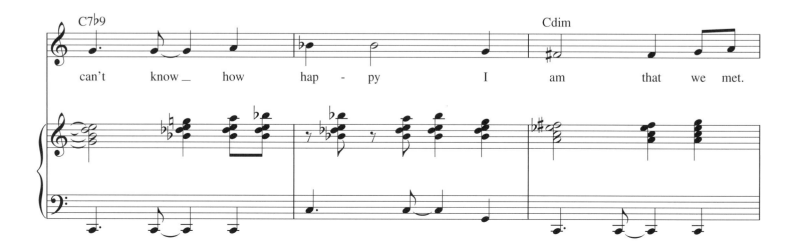

can't know _ how hap - py I am that we met.

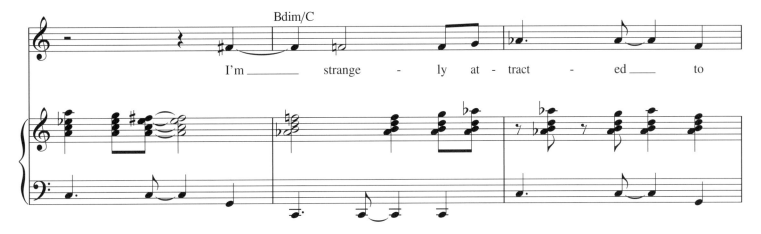

I'm _____ strange - ly at - tract - ed _____ to

you. There's some - one ___ I'm

try - ing ___ so hard to for - get;

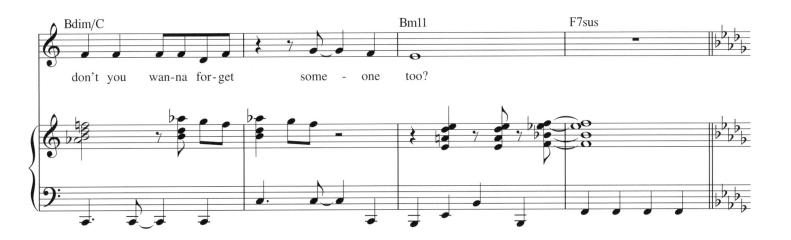

don't you wan-na for-get some - one too?

Wrong game, _____ with the wrong chips. Though your

lips are tempt - ing, they're the wrong ___ lips.

They're not her chops, _ but they're such

tempt - ing chops that if some night _ you might _ be

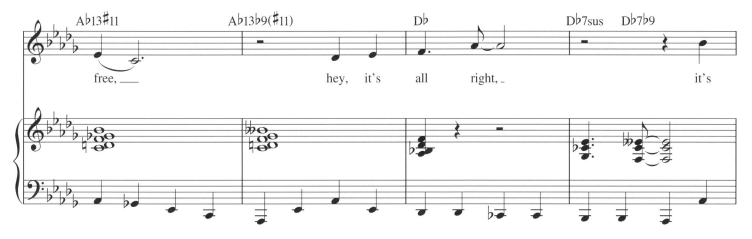

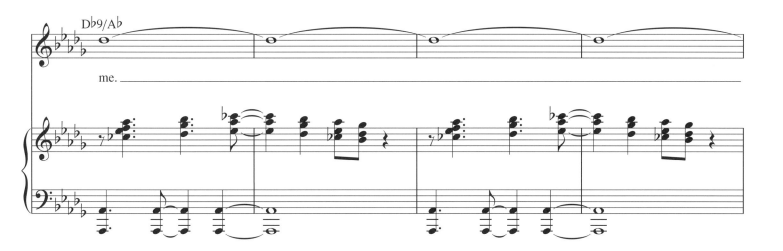

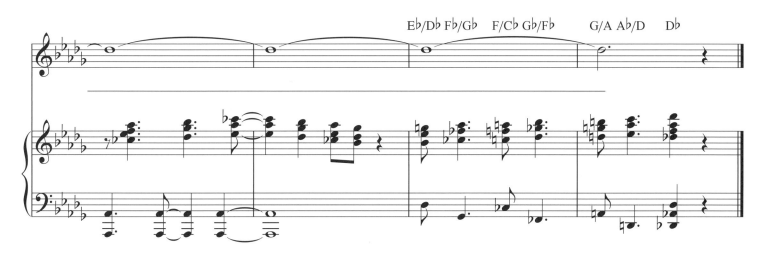

JUST FRIENDS

Lyrics by SAM M. LEWIS
Music by JOHN KLENNER

Moderately slow Ballad

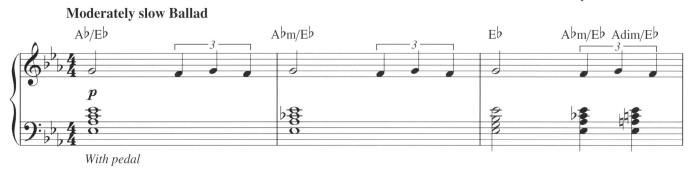

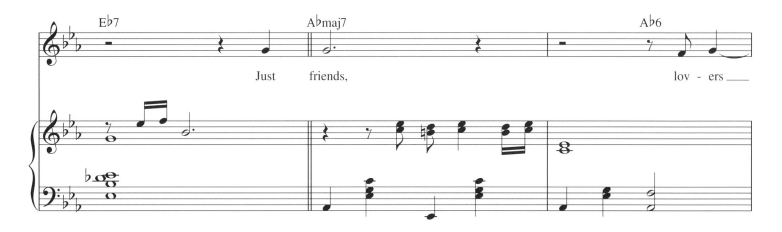

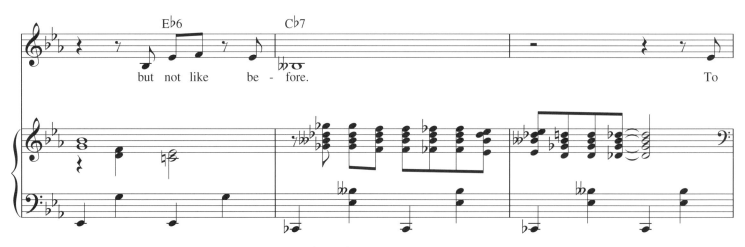

© 1931 (Renewed) METRO-GOLDWYN-MAYER, INC.
All Rights Controlled and Administered by EMI ROBBINS CATALOG INC. (Publishing) and ALFRED PUBLISHING CO., INC. (Print)
All Rights Reserved   Used by Permission

think of what we've been, and not to kiss a-gain,

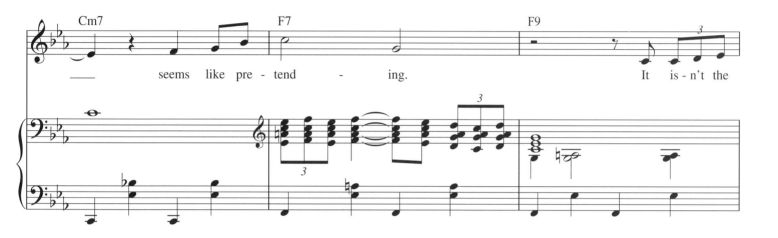

seems like pre-tend - ing. It is-n't the

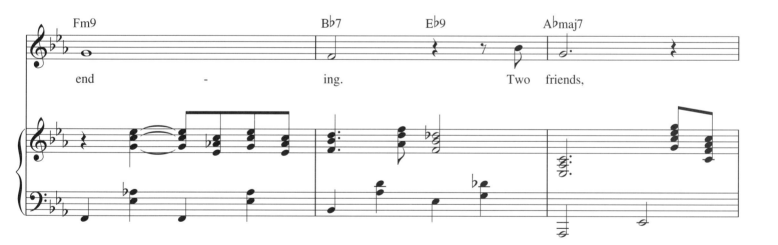

end - ing. Two friends,

drift - ing a - part. Two

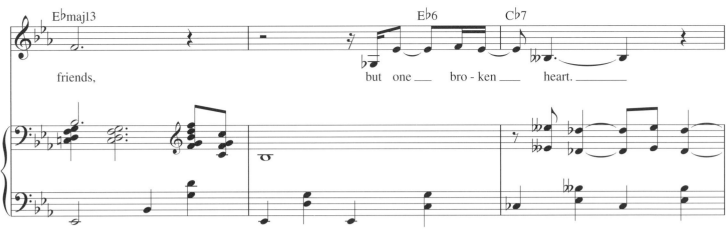

friends, but one ___ bro - ken ___ heart. ___

We loved, we laughed, we cried;

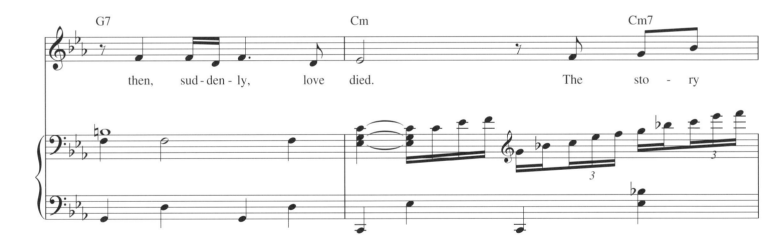

then, sud - den - ly, love died. The sto - ry

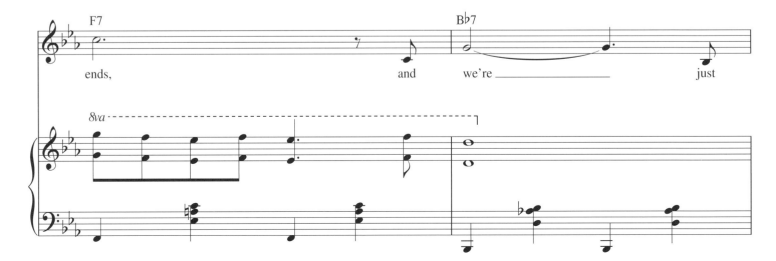

ends, and we're _____ just

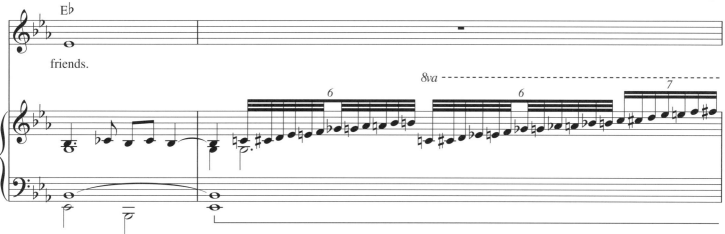

friends.

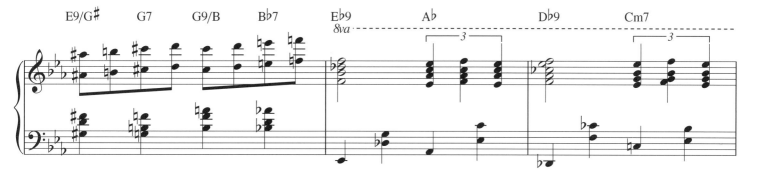

We

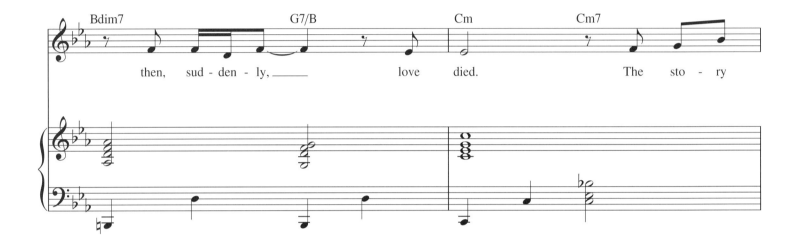

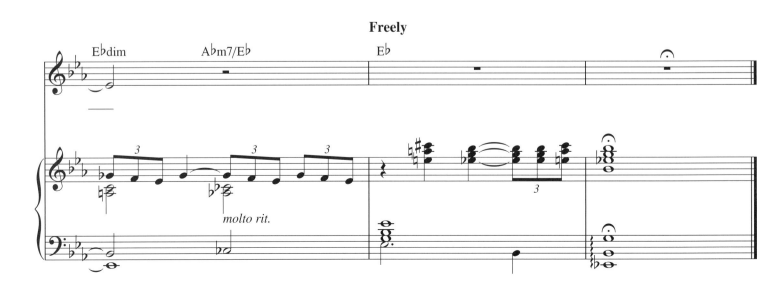

LEAN BABY

Lyric by ROY ALFRED
Music by BILLY MAY

© 1952, 1953 (Renewed) MORLEY MUSIC CO.
All Rights Reserved

I know I love her so, I'll nev-er ev-er let her go, no! ___

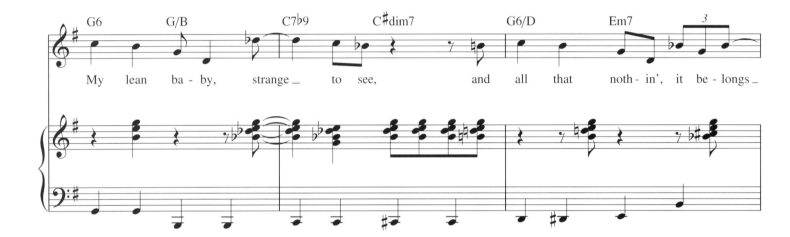

My lean ba-by, strange ___ to see, and all that noth-in', it be-longs ___

___ to me, ___ and though she may be scrawn-y, she's ___

___ o-kay, be-cause I would-n't want her an-y oth-er way. ___

And ___ she's so skin-ny, she's ___ so drawn, when

she stands side-ways ___ you would think that she's gone. ___ But

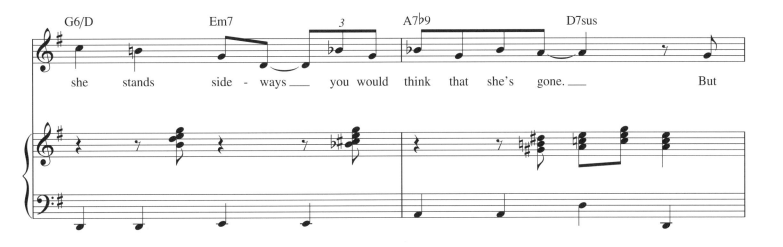

when she calls me, ___ "Ba-by," I _____ feel fine ___ to think she's fran-tic-'ly, ro-man-tic-'ly mine. _

I _____ chased her ___ and I caught her, then a

dia - mond ring ___ I ___ bought her. Hey, ___ the dia-monds shine, the

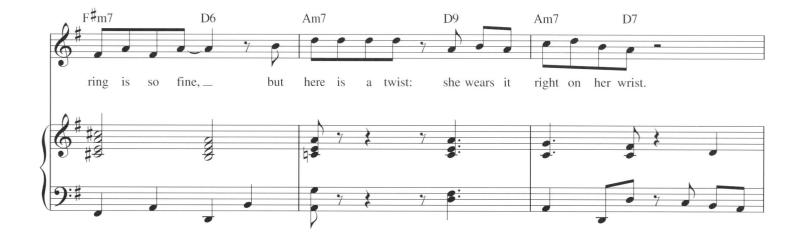

ring is so fine, ___ but here is a twist: she wears it right on her wrist.

My lean ba - by, she's ___ so slim. A broom - stick's wid - er, but

not as trim, and when she starts to kiss me, then ___ I know I love her

LEARNIN' THE BLUES

Words and Music by
DOLORES "VICKI" SILVERS

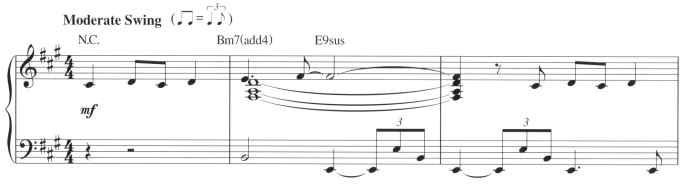

The ta-bles are

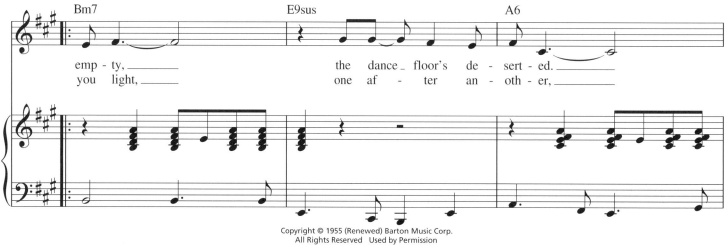

emp-ty, _____ the dance floor's de-sert-ed. _____
you light, _____ one af-ter an-oth-er, _____

Copyright © 1955 (Renewed) Barton Music Corp.
All Rights Reserved   Used by Permission

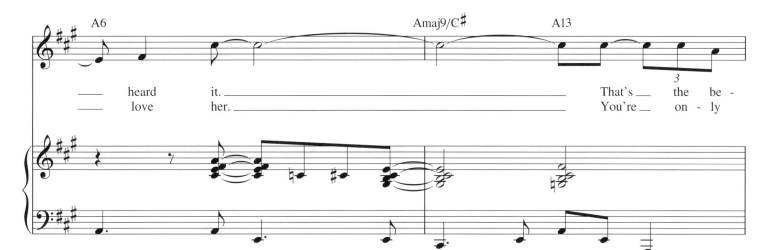

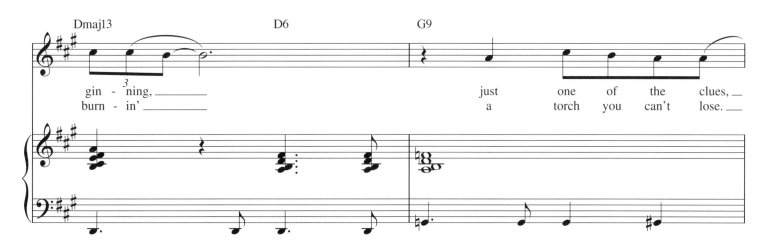

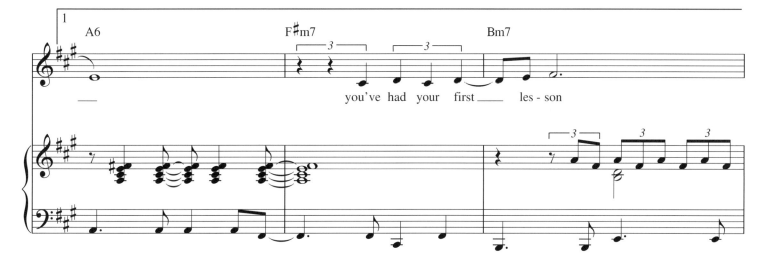

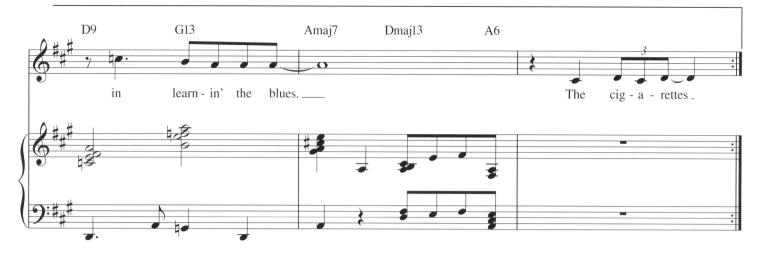

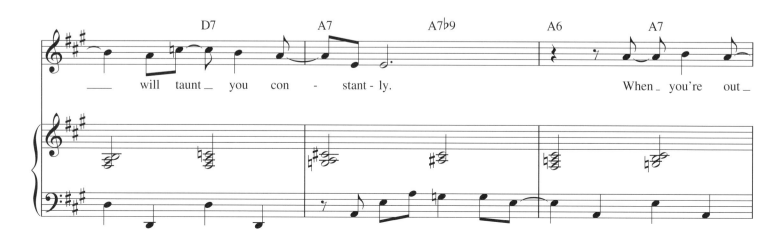

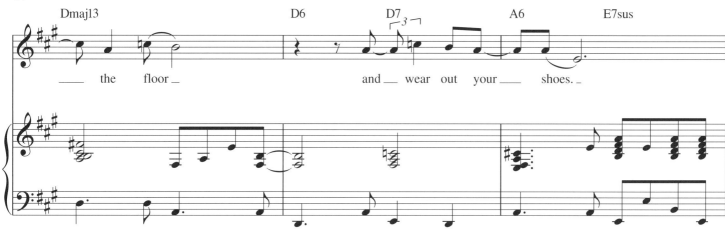

the floor and wear out your shoes.

When you feel your heart break, you're learn-

in' the blues.

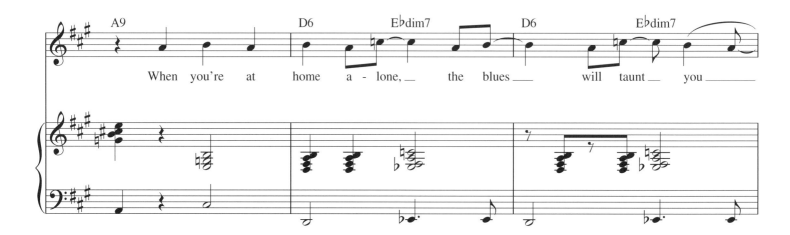

When you're at home a - lone, the blues will taunt you

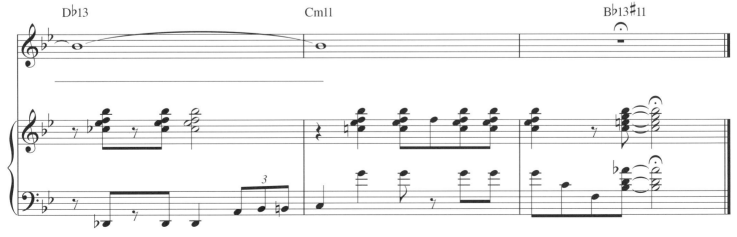

MAKIN' WHOOPEE!

Lyrics by GUS KAHN
Music by WALTER DONALDSON

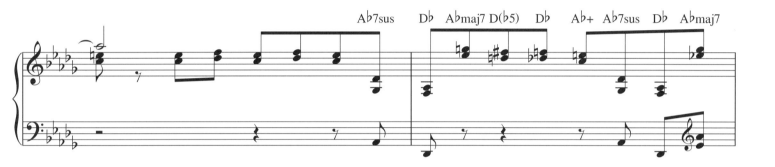

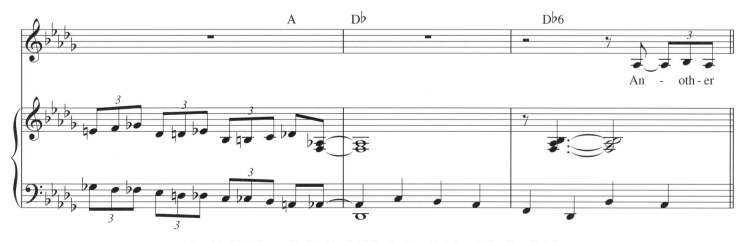

An - oth - er

Copyright © 1928 (Renewed) by Donaldson Publishing Co., Dreyer Music Co. and Gilbert Keyes Music Co.
All Rights for Dreyer Music Co. Administered by Larry Spier, Inc., New York
International Copyright Secured   All Rights Reserved

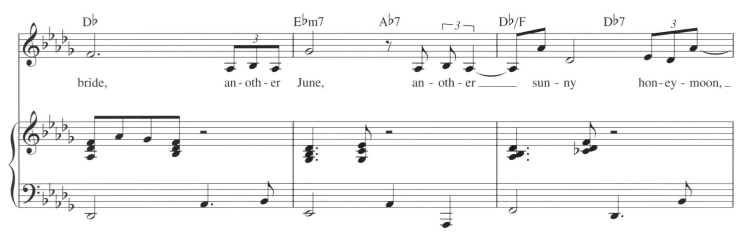

bride, an - oth - er June, an - oth - er _____ sun - ny hon - ey - moon, _

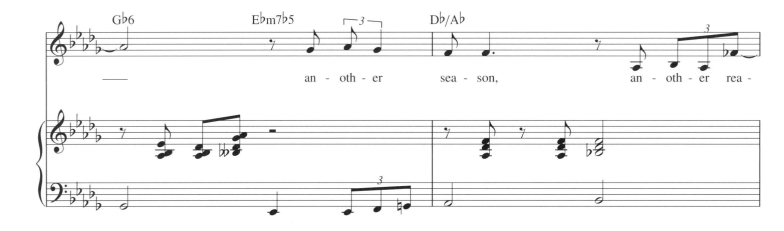

_____ an - oth - er sea - son, an - oth - er rea -

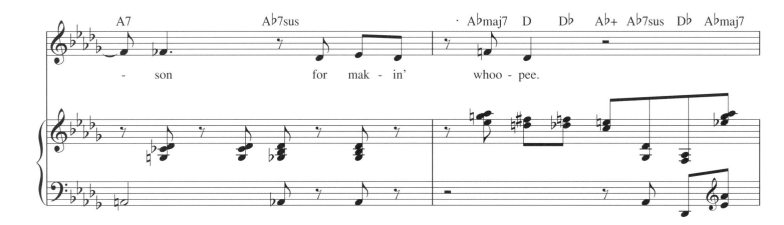

- son for mak - in' whoo - pee.

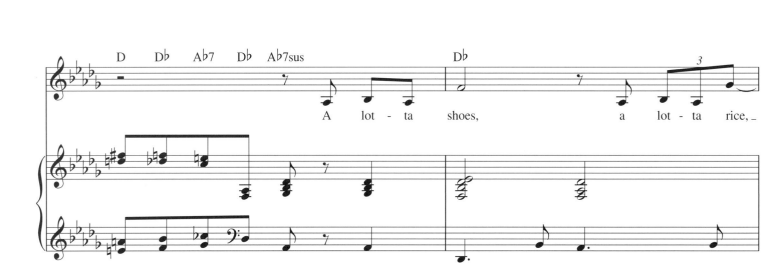

A lot - ta shoes, a lot - ta rice, _

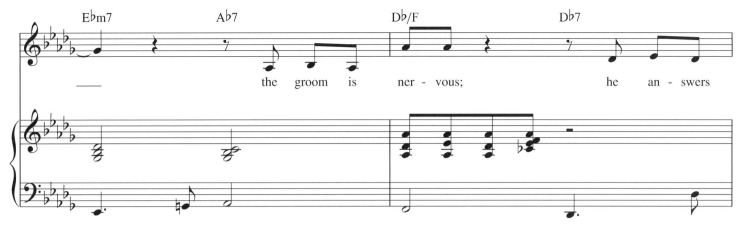

the groom is ner - vous; he an - swers

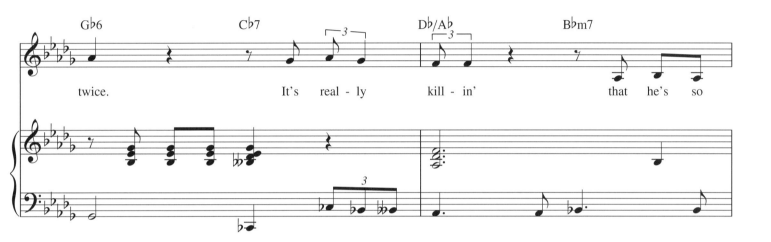

twice. It's real - ly kill - in' that he's so

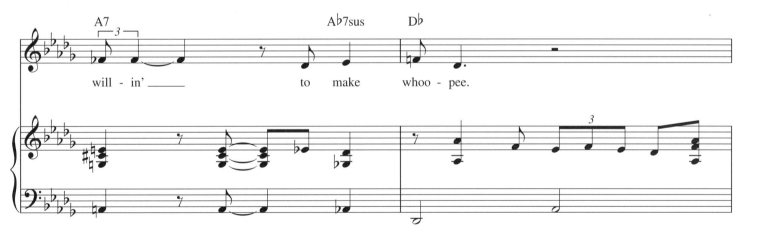

will - in' to make whoo - pee.

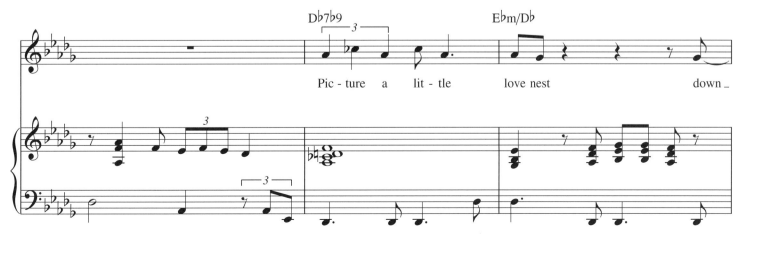

Pic - ture a lit - tle love nest down

where the ros - es cling. ___ Pic - ture the same ___ sweet love ___

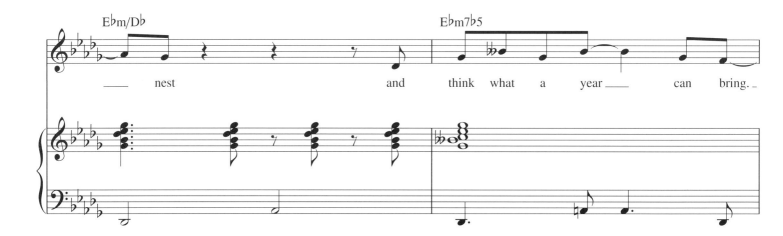

nest and think what a year ___ can bring.

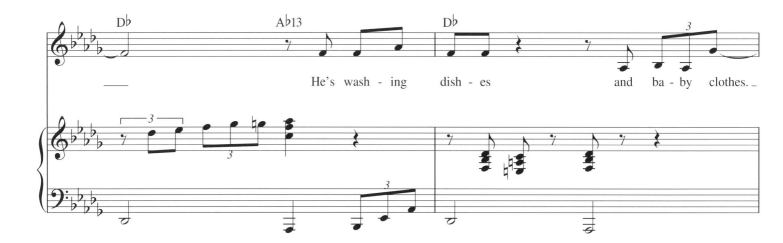

He's wash - ing dish - es and ba - by clothes. ___

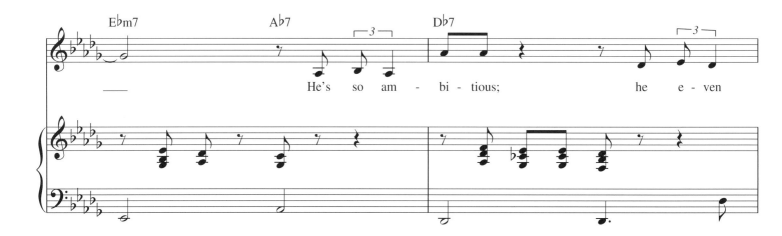

He's so am - bi - tious; he e - ven

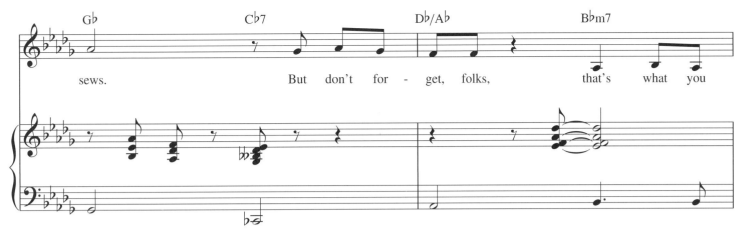

sews. But don't for - get, folks, that's what you

get, folks, for mak - in' whoo - pee.

An - oth - er bride, _____ an - oth - er June, _

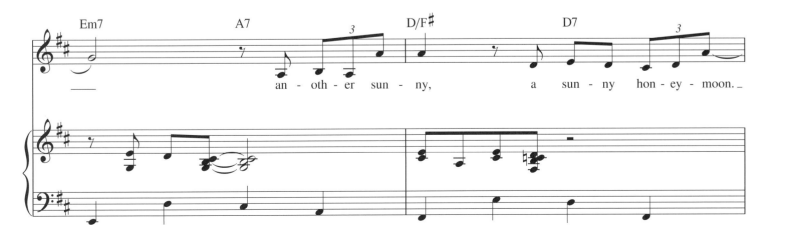

_____ an - oth - er sun - ny, a sun - ny hon - ey - moon. _

An - oth - er rea - son is that

sea - son for mak - in' whoo - pee.

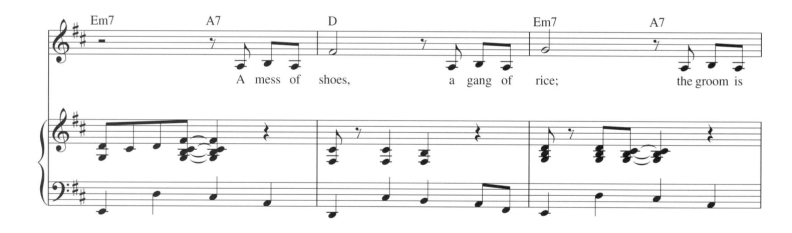

A mess of shoes, a gang of rice; the groom is

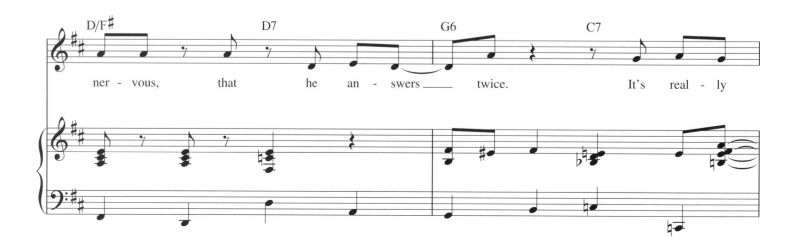

ner - vous, that he an - swers twice. It's real - ly

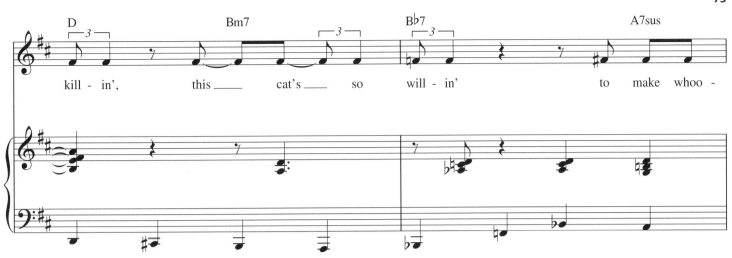

kill - in', this ___ cat's ___ so will - in' to make whoo -

pee.

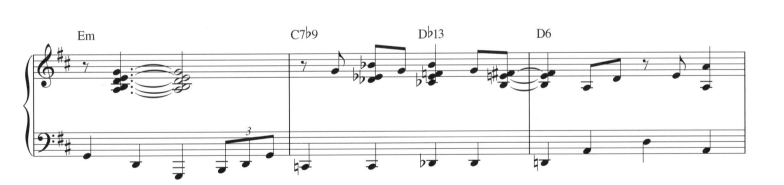

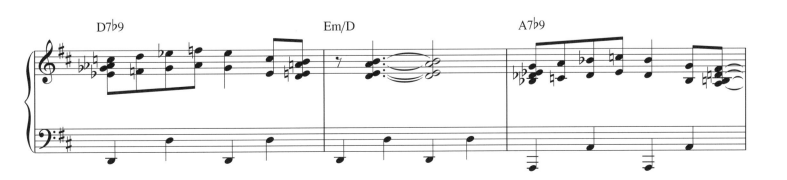

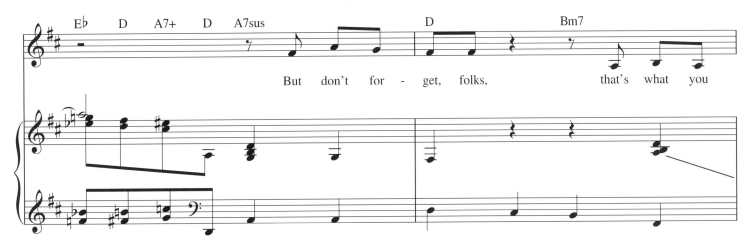

But don't for - get, folks,   that's what you

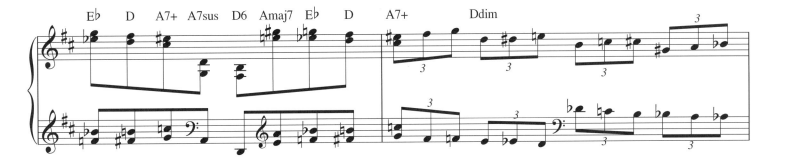

get, folks,   for mak - in' whoo - pee. _____

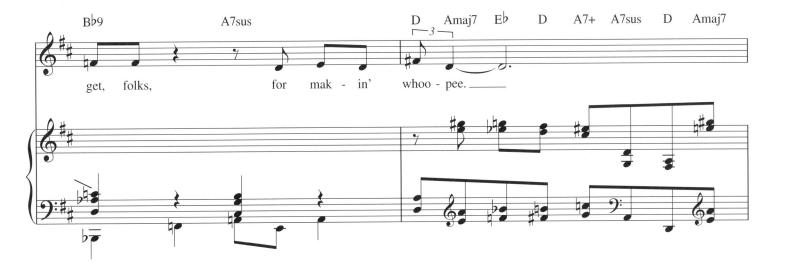

LET'S FACE THE MUSIC AND DANCE

Words and Music by
IRVING BERLIN

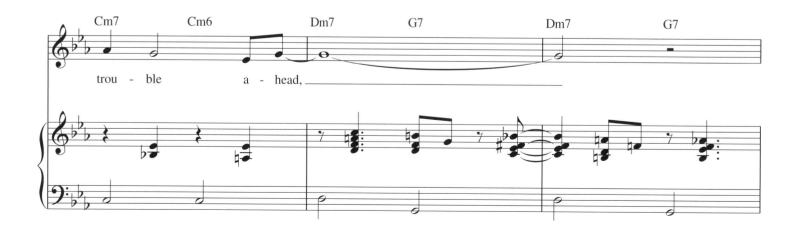

© Copyright 1935, 1936 by Irving Berlin
Copyright Renewed
International Copyright Secured   All Rights Reserved

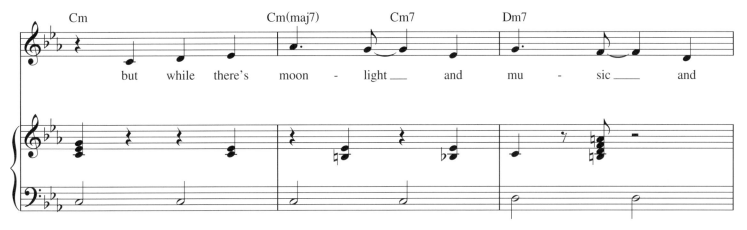

but while there's moon - light ____ and mu - sic ____ and

love and ___ ro - mance,

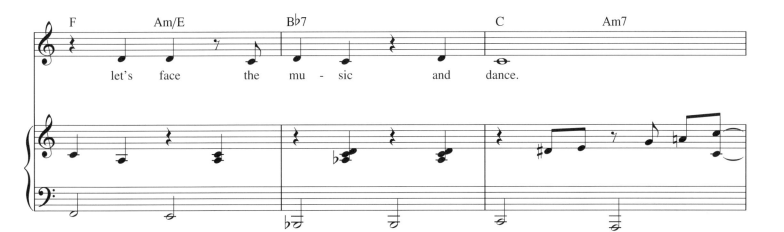

let's face the mu - sic and dance.

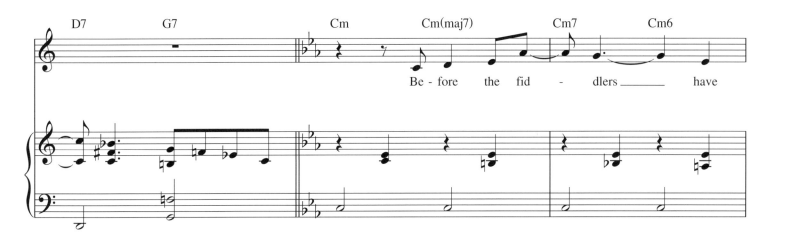

Be - fore the fid - dlers _____ have

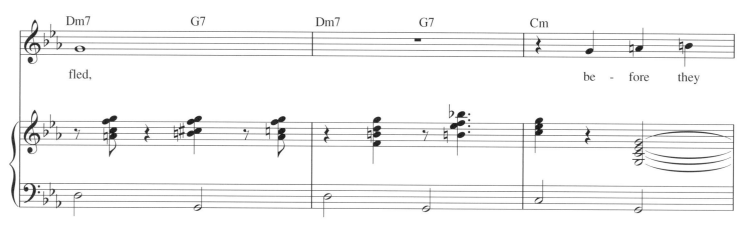

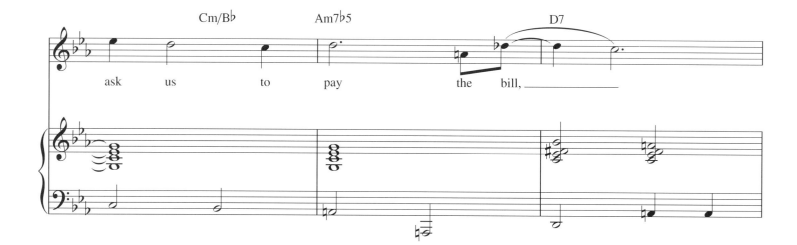

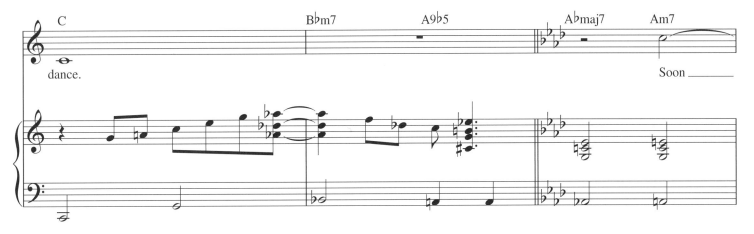

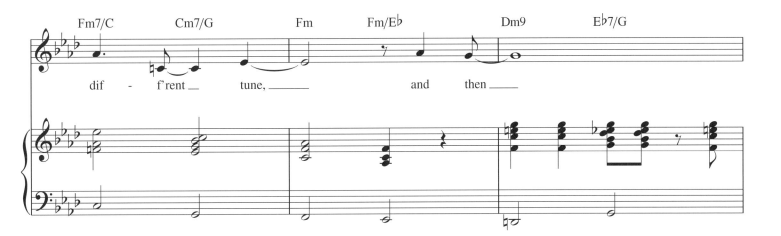

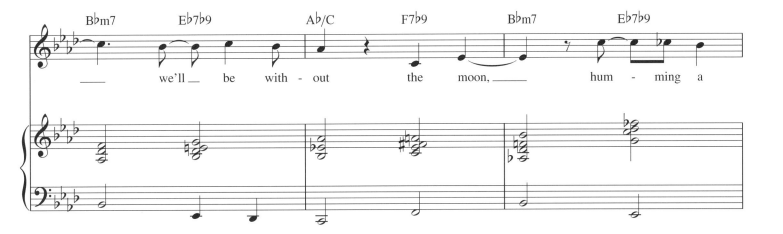

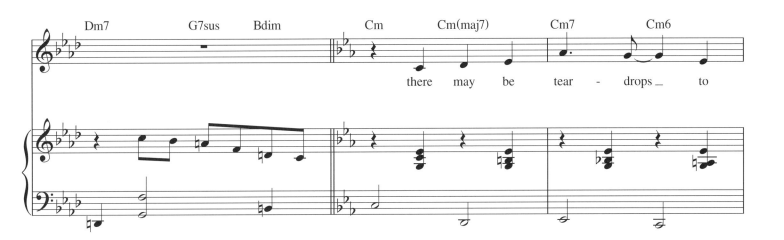

shed. So while there's

moon - light __ and mu - sic __ and love __ and ro - mance, __

__ face the

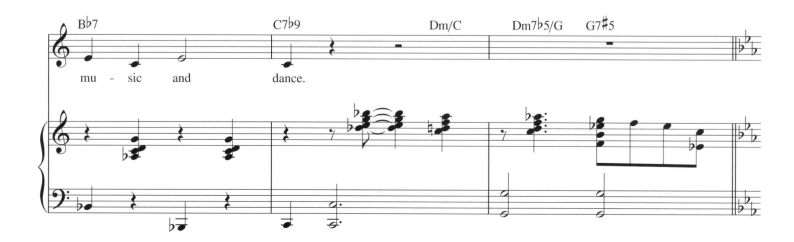

mu - sic and dance.

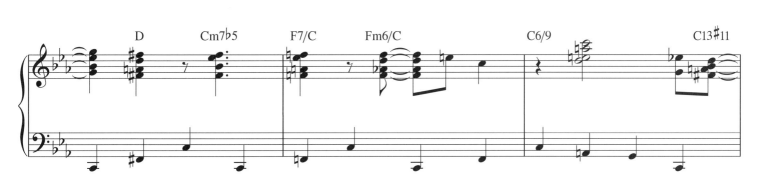

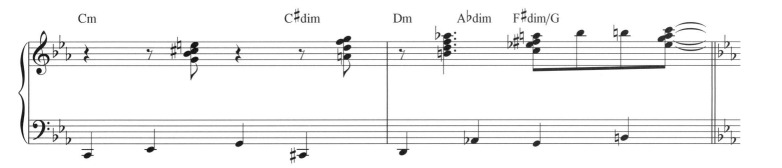

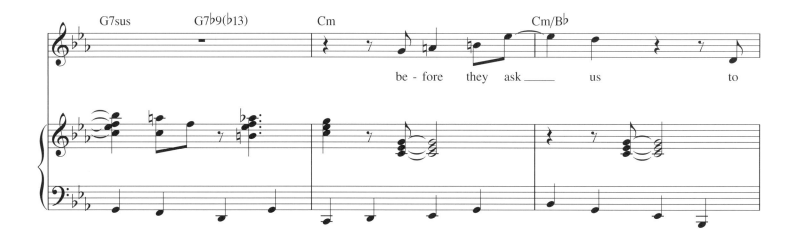

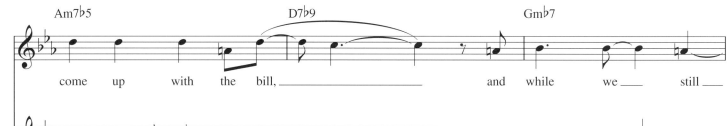

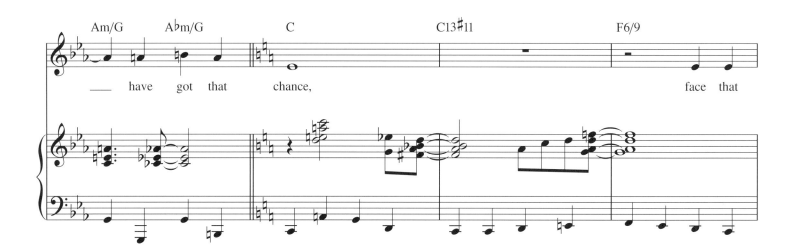

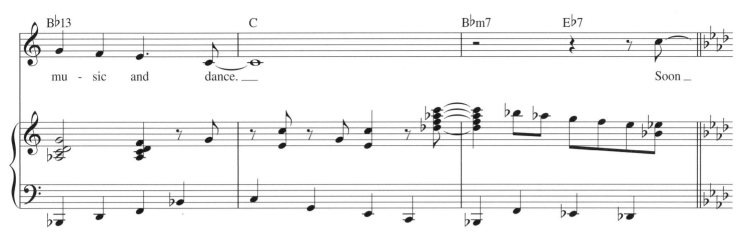

mu - sic and dance. ___ Soon ___

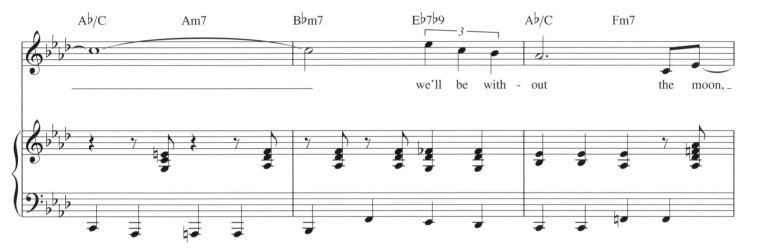

we'll be with - out the moon, ___

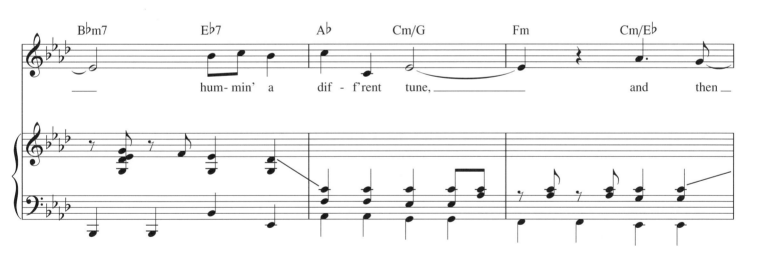

___ hum - min' a dif - f'rent tune, ___ and then ___

there may be ___

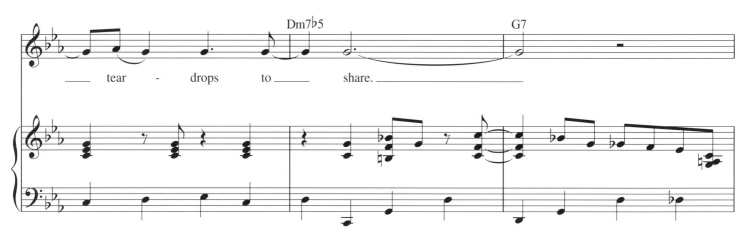

tear - drops to ___ share. _____

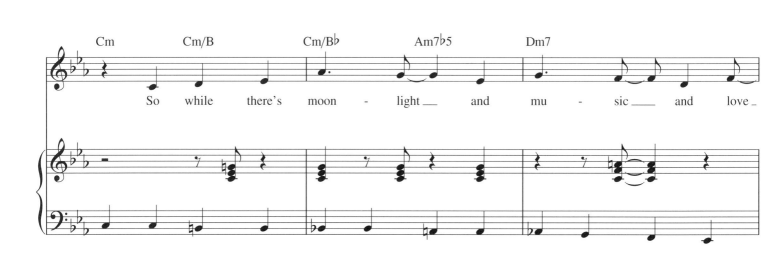

So while there's moon - light ___ and mu - sic ___ and love _

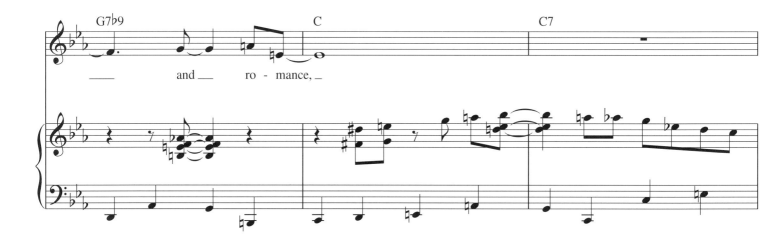

___ and ___ ro - mance, _

let's face the mu - sic and dance, ___

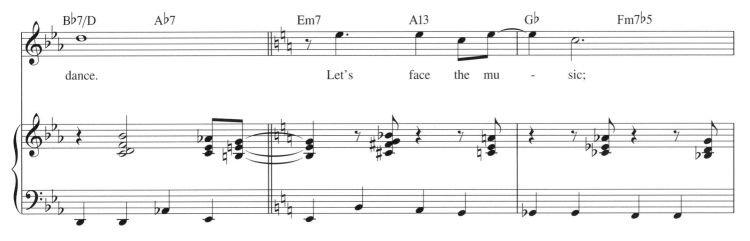

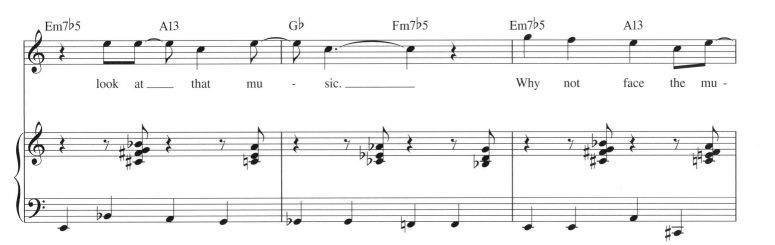

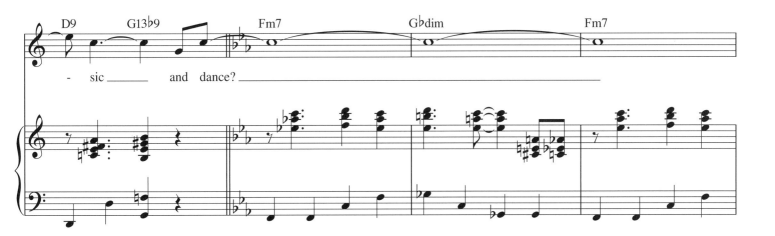

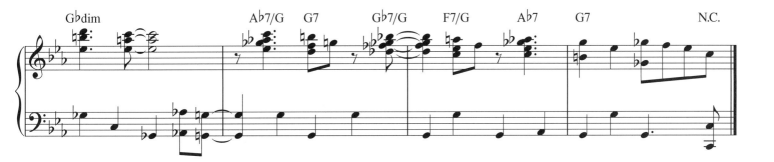

LET'S FALL IN LOVE

Words by TED KOEHLER
Music by HAROLD ARLEN

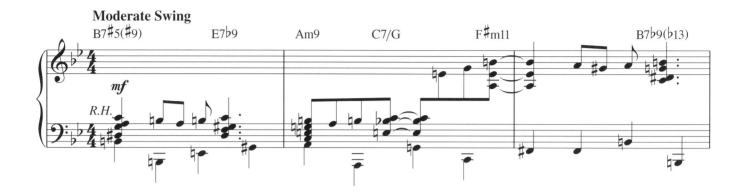

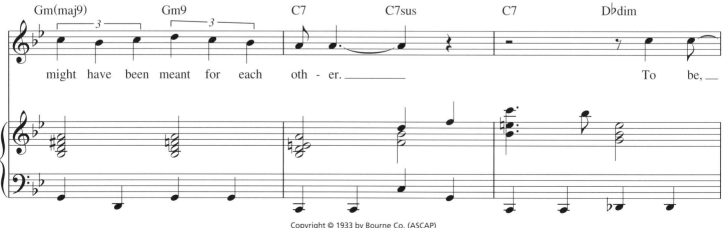

Copyright © 1933 by Bourne Co. (ASCAP)
Copyright Renewed
International Copyright Secured   All Rights Reserved

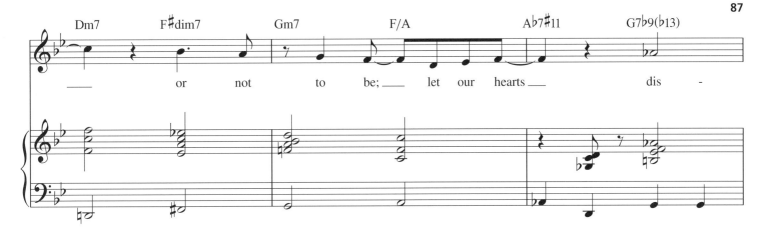

or not to be; ___ let our hearts ___ dis -

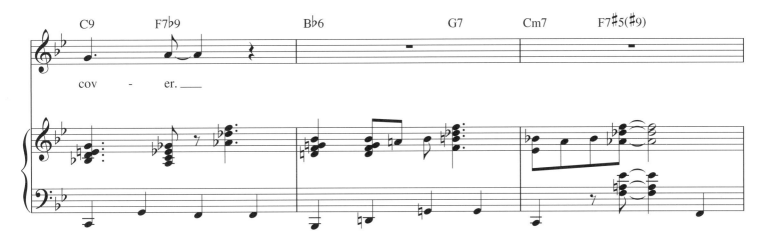

cov - er. ___

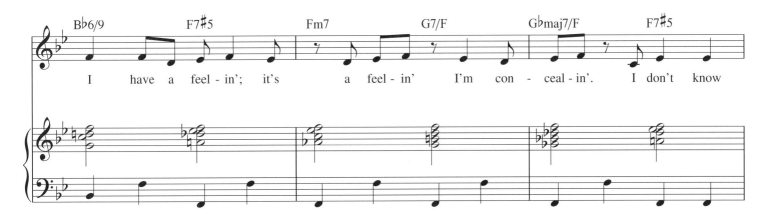

I have a feel - in'; it's a feel - in' I'm con - ceal - in'. I don't know

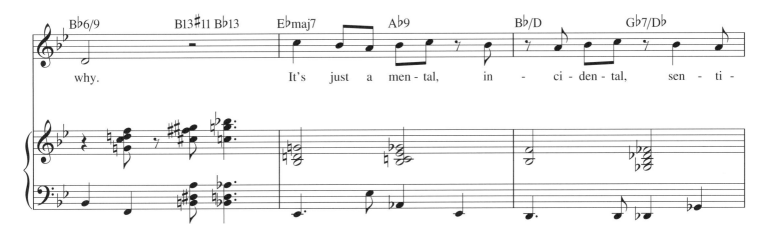

why. It's just a men - tal, in - ci - den - tal, sen - ti -

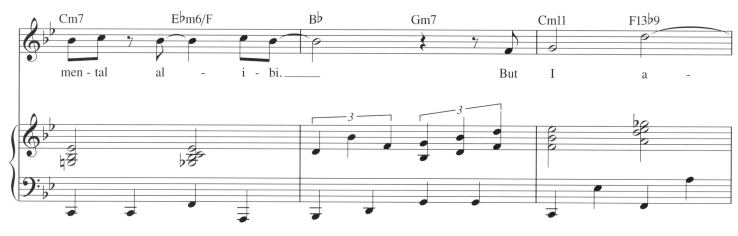

men - tal al - i - bi._____ But I a -

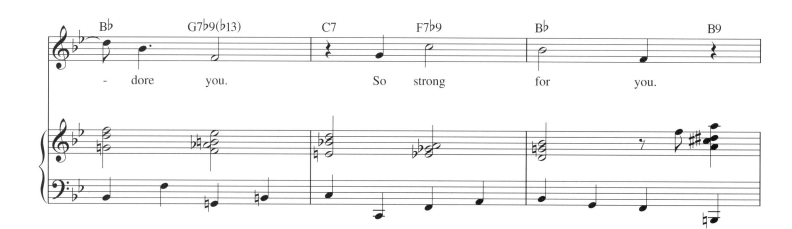

- dore you. So strong for you.

Why go on stall - in'? I_____ am fall - in'. Love is call - in.' Why be

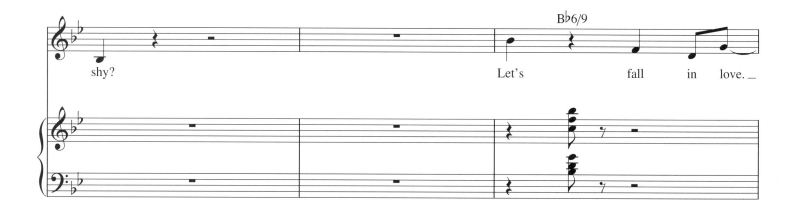

shy? Let's fall in love.__

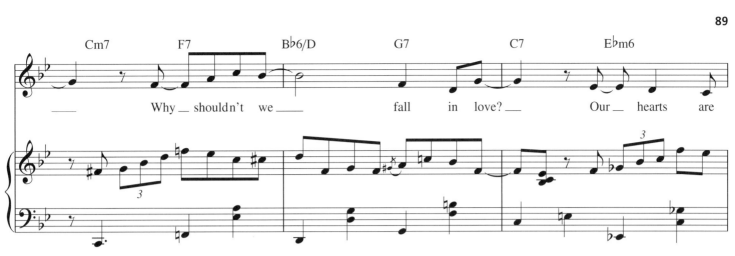

Why — shouldn't we — fall in love? — Our — hearts are

made of it; let's take a chance; why — be a-fraid — of it?

Let's close _____ our eyes ___ and — make our —

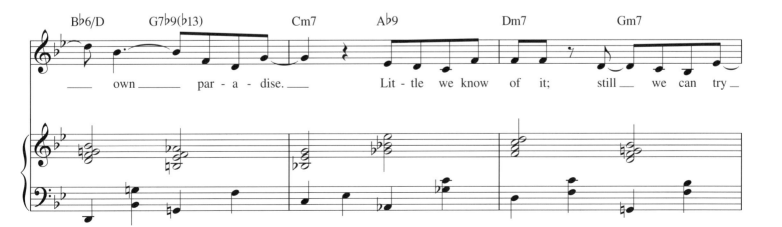

___ own _____ par - a - dise. ___ Lit - tle we know of it; still ___ we can try —

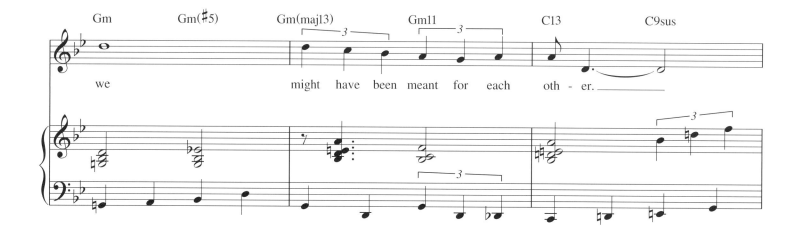

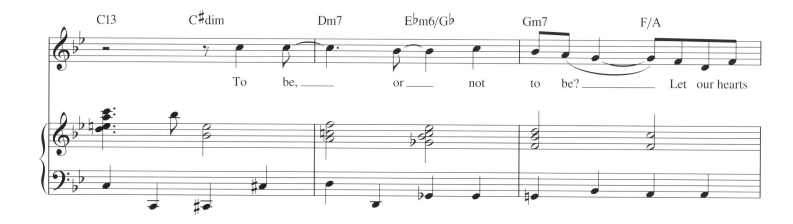

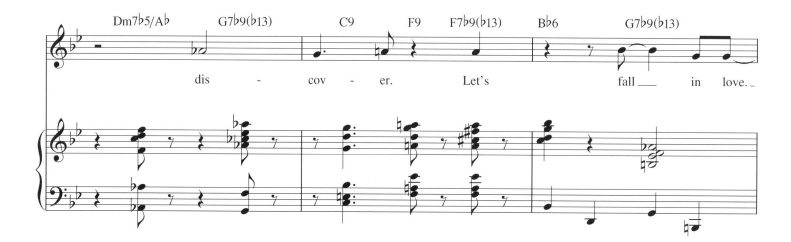

MOONLIGHT BECOMES YOU

Words by JOHNNY BURKE
Music by JAMES VAN HEUSEN

Moderately slow, expressively

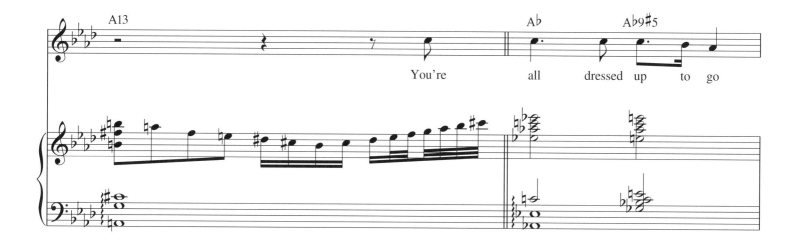

Copyright © 1942 Sony/ATV Music Publishing LLC
Copyright Renewed
All Rights Administered by Sony/ATV Music Publishing LLC, 8 Music Square West, Nashville, TN 37203
International Copyright Secured   All Rights Reserved

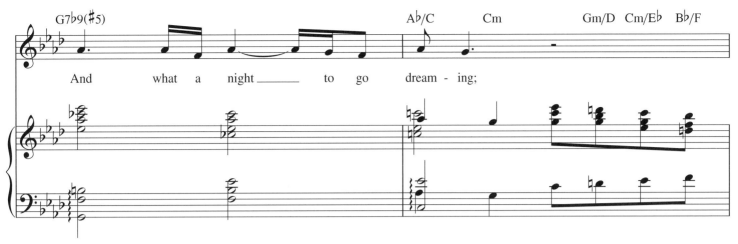

And what a night____ to go dream - ing;

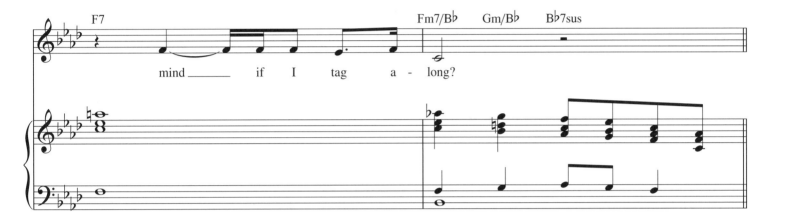

mind____ if I tag a - long?

Moderately slow, steady Ballad

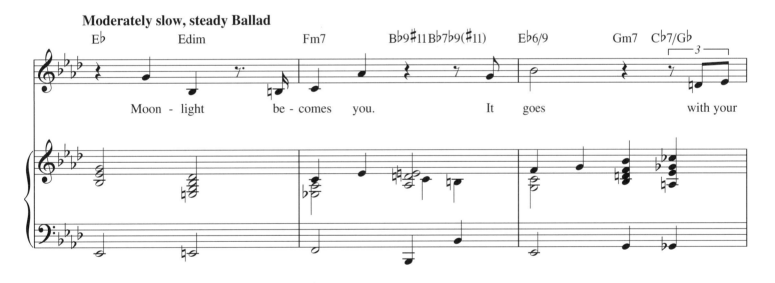

Moon - light be - comes you. It goes with your

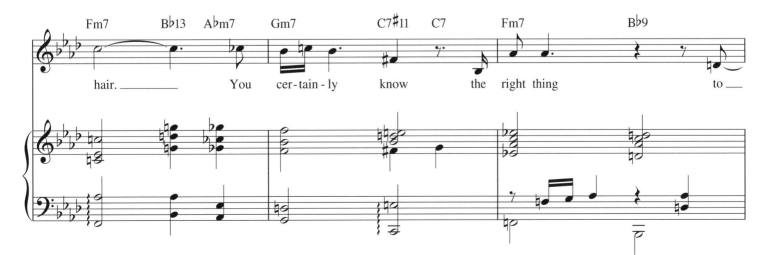

hair.____ You cer - tain - ly know the right thing to __

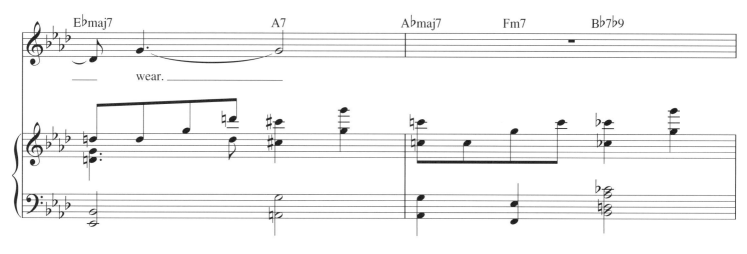

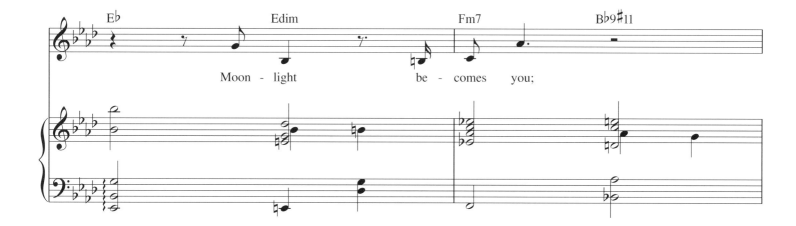

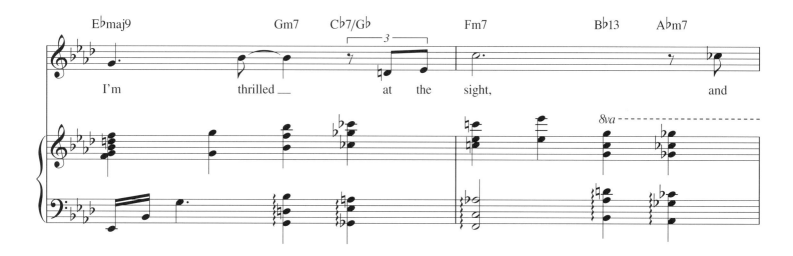

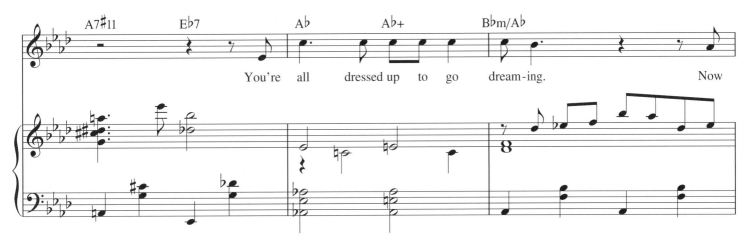

You're all dressed up to go dream-ing. Now

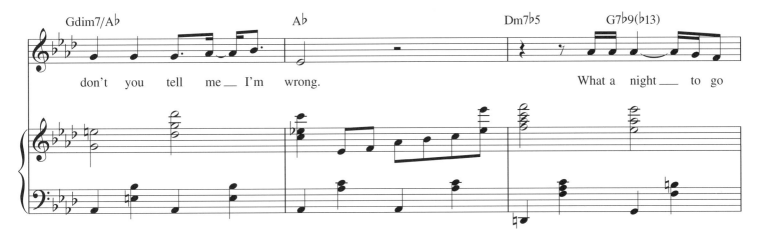

don't you tell me ___ I'm wrong. What a night ___ to go

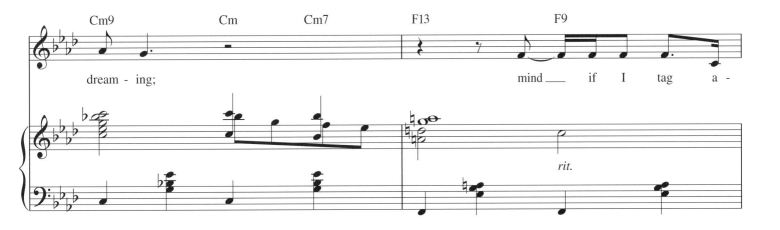

dream - ing; mind ___ if I tag a-

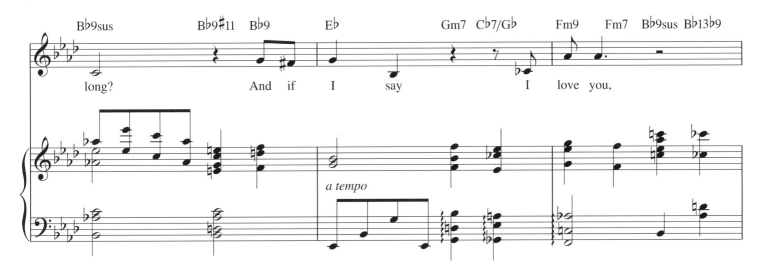

long? And if I say I love you,

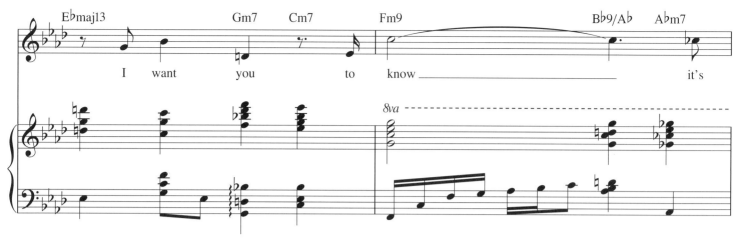

I want you to know _____ it's

not just be-cause _ there's moon-light. Al-though

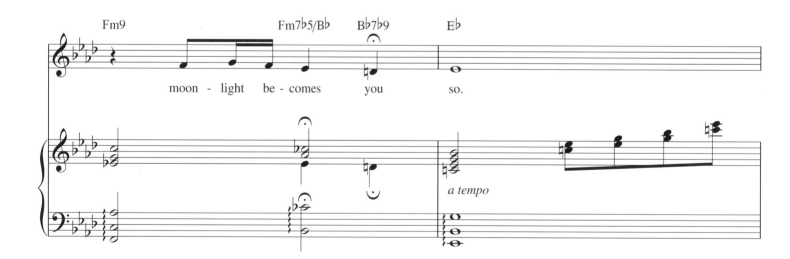

moon-light be-comes you so.

Very expressively

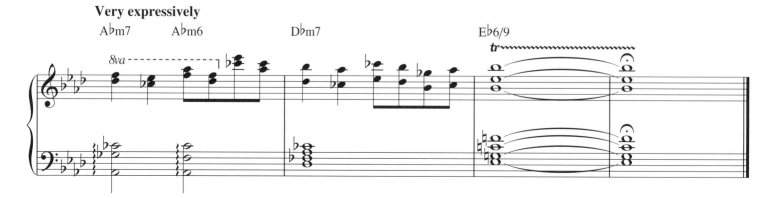

MY WAY

English Words by PAUL ANKA
Original French Words by GILLES THIBAULT
Music by JACQUES REVAUX and CLAUDE FRANCOIS

Copyright © 1967 Societe Des Nouvelles and Editions Eddie Barclay
Copyright © 1969 Chrysalis Standards, Inc.
Copyright Renewed
All Rights for the USA Administered by Chrysalis Standards, Inc., Editions Jeune Musique, Warner Chappell Music France, Jingoro Co. and Architectural Music Co.
All Rights Reserved   Used by Permission

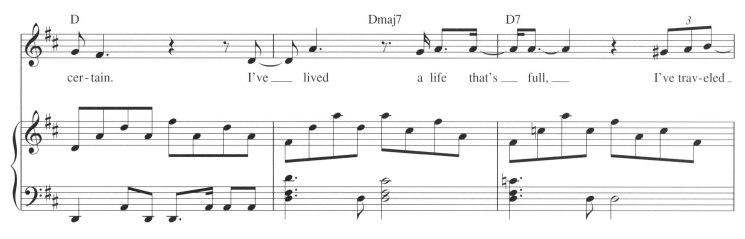

cer - tain. I've __ lived a life that's __ full, __ I've trav-eled __

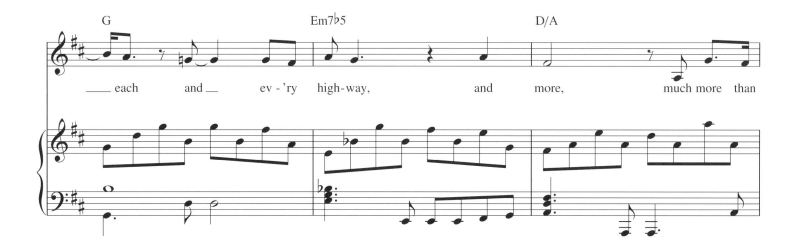

__ each and __ ev-'ry high-way, and more, much more than

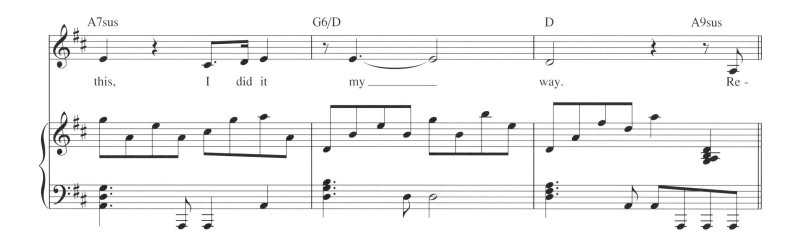

this, I did it my _____ way. Re -

grets, I've __ had a few, but then a - gain, __ too __ few to
loved, I've __ laughed and cried. I've had my fill, ___ my __ share of

men-tion. I did what I ___ had to do, and saw it
los-ing. And now, as ___ tears sub-side, I find it

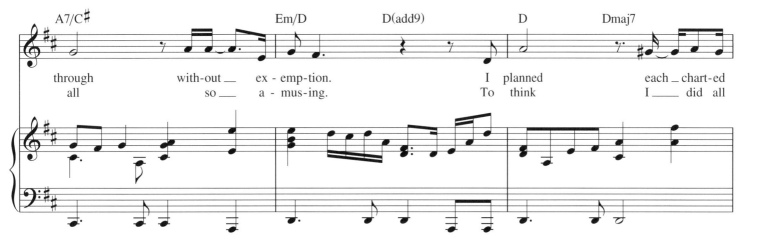

through with-out ___ ex-emp-tion. I planned each ___ chart-ed
all so ___ a-mus-ing. To think I ___ did all

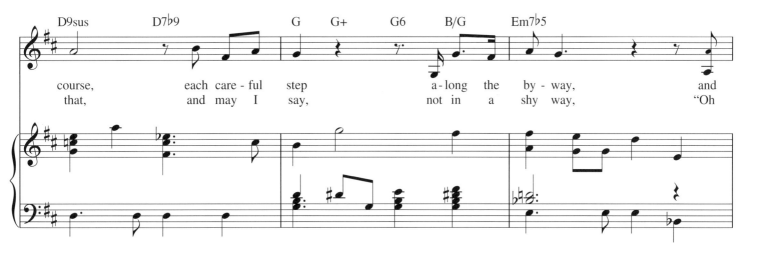

course, each care-ful step a-long the by-way, and
that, and may I say, not in a shy way, "Oh

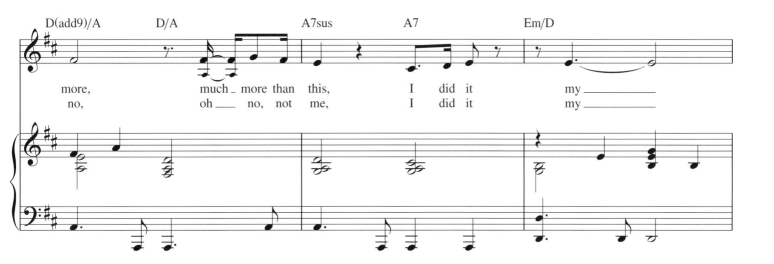

more, much ___ more than this, I did it my ___
no, oh ___ no, not me, I did it my ___

way. Yes, there were times, I'm sure you knew, when I
way." For what is a man? What has he got? If not

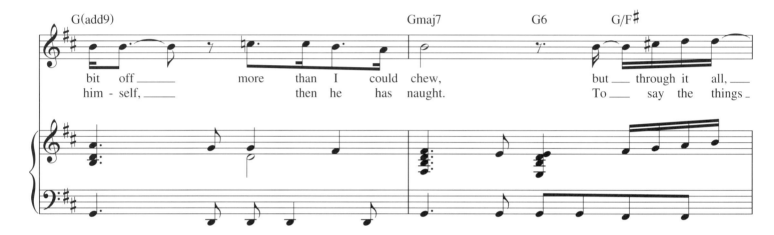

bit off _____ more than I could chew, but _____ through it all, _____
him-self, _____ then he has naught. To _____ say the things _____

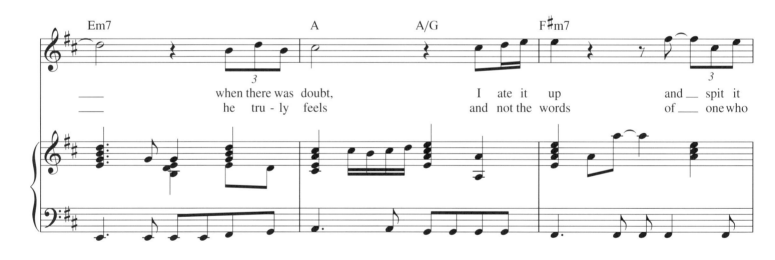

_____ when there was doubt, I ate it up and _____ spit it
_____ he tru-ly feels and not the words of _____ one who

To Coda ⊕

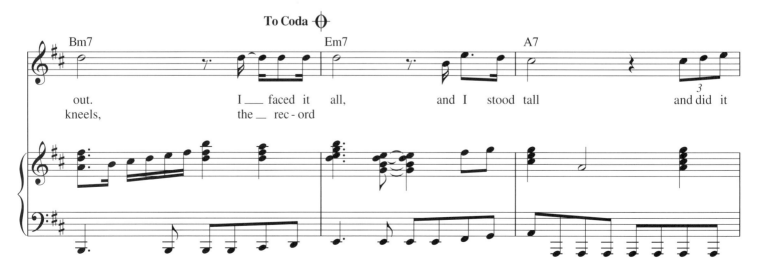

out. I _____ faced it all, and I stood tall and did it
kneels, the _____ rec-ord

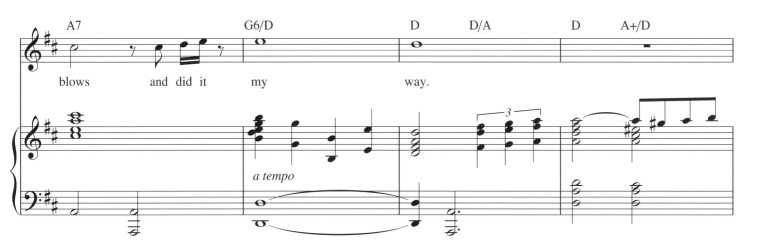

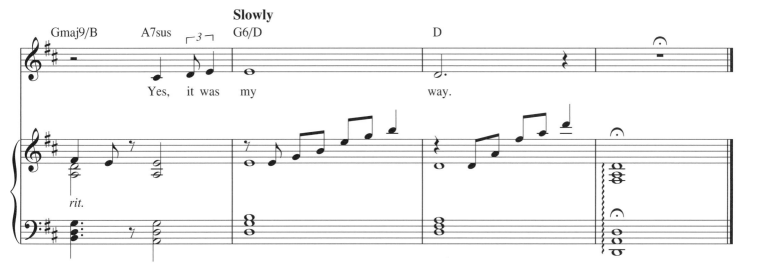

MY FUNNY VALENTINE

Words by LORENZ HART
Music by RICHARD RODGERS

Copyright ©1937 (Renewed) by Chappell & Co.
Rights for the Extended Renewal Term in the U.S. Controlled by Williamson Music and WB Music Corp. o/b/o The Estate Of Lorenz Hart
International Copyright Secured   All Rights Reserved

Your looks are laugh - a - ble, un -

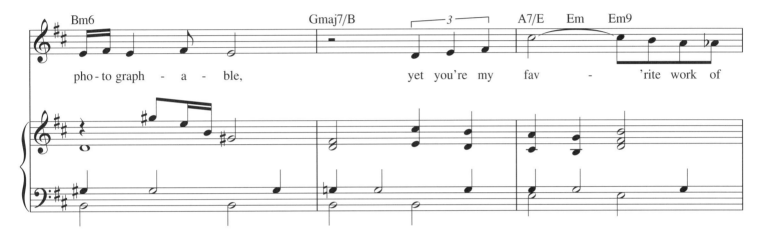

pho - to graph - a - ble, yet you're my fav - 'rite work of

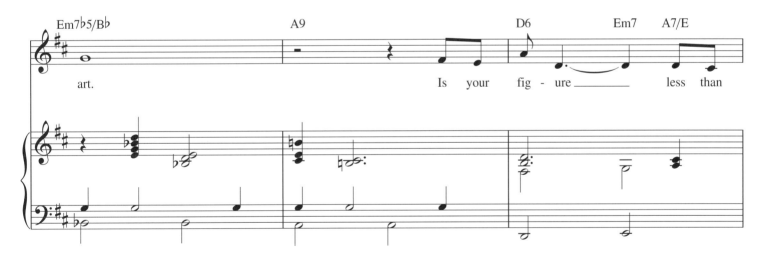

art. Is your fig - ure _____ less than

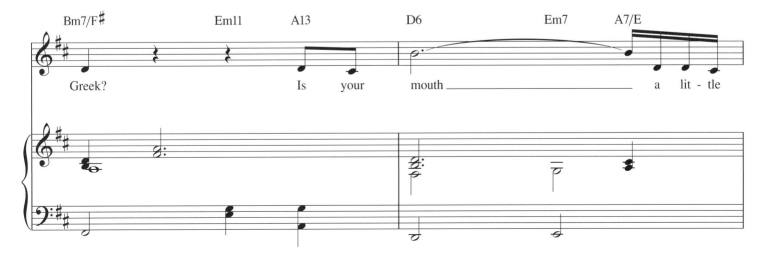

Greek? Is your mouth _____ a lit - tle

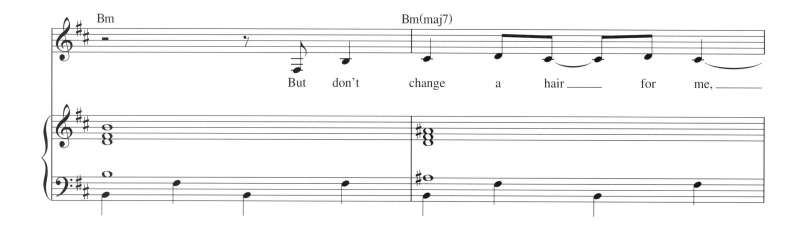

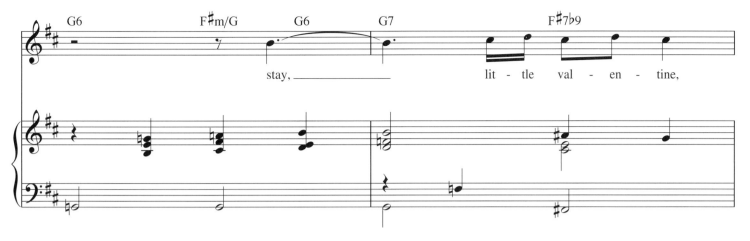

stay, _____ lit - tle val - en - tine,

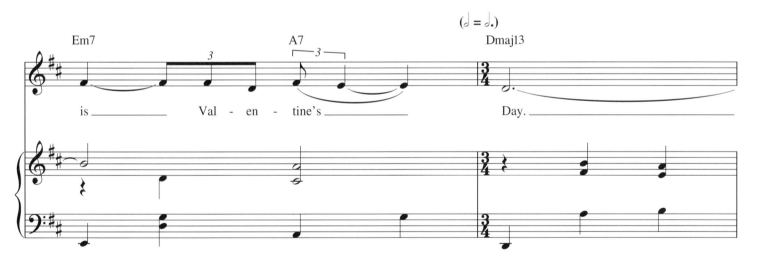

stay. _____ Each day

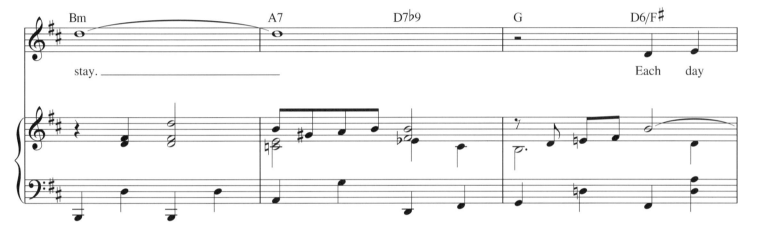

is _____ Val - en - tine's _____ Day.

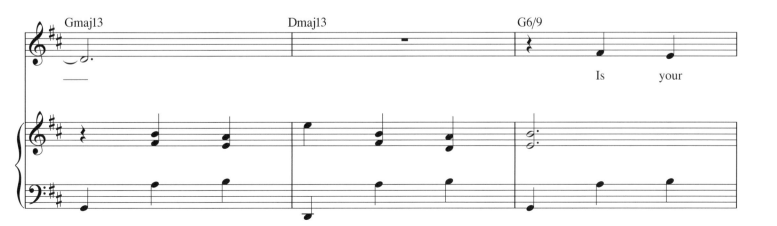

____ Is your

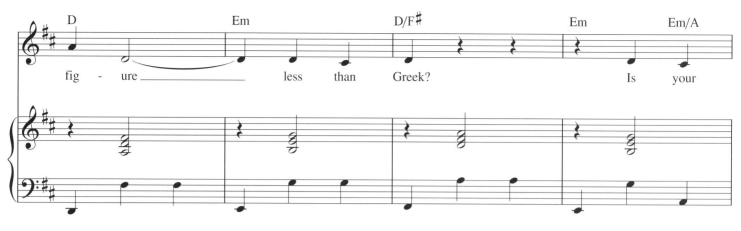

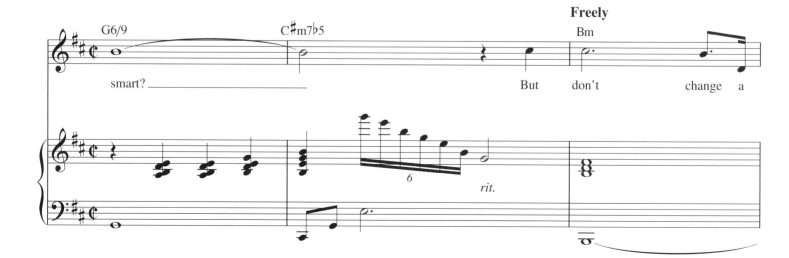

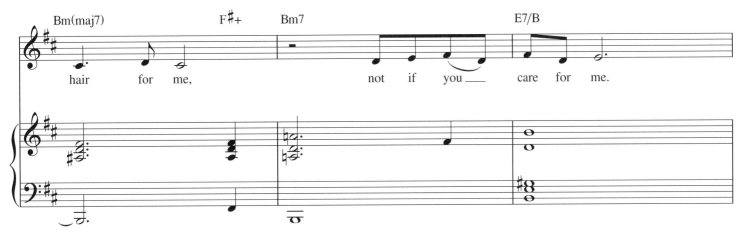

hair for me, not if you ___ care for me.

Tempo I

Stay, ___ lit - tle val - en - tine, ___ stay. ___

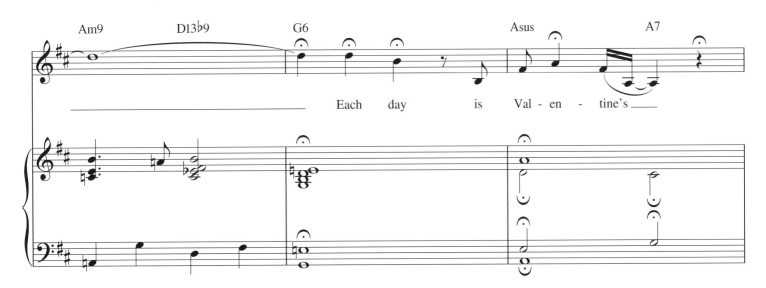

___ Each day is Val - en - tine's ___

Slowly, freely

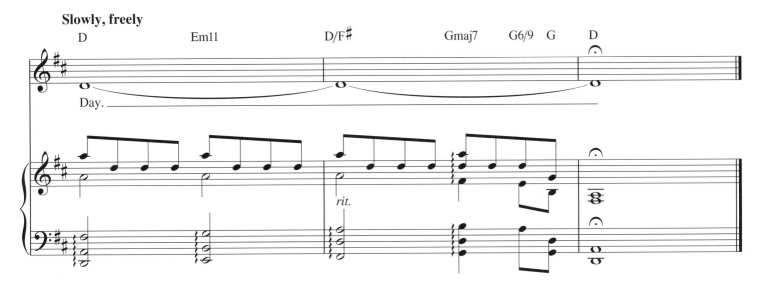

Day. ___

THEME FROM
"NEW YORK, NEW YORK"

Words by FRED EBB
Music by JOHN KANDER

© 1977 (Renewed) UNITED ARTISTS CORPORATION
All Rights Controlled and Administered by EMI UNART CATALOG INC. (Publishing) and ALFRED PUBLISHING CO., INC. (Print)
All Rights Reserved   Used by Permission

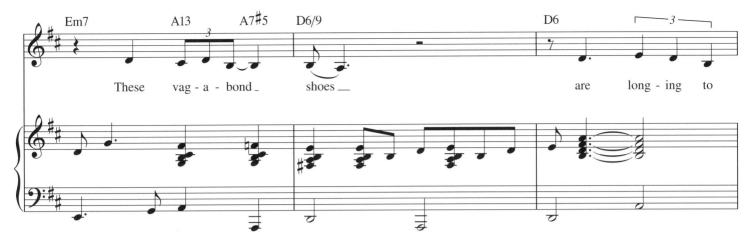

These vag-a-bond shoes are long-ing to

stray right through the ver-y heart of it,

New York, New York. I wan-na

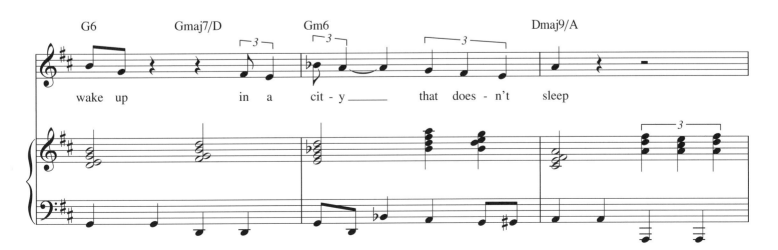

wake up in a cit-y that does-n't sleep

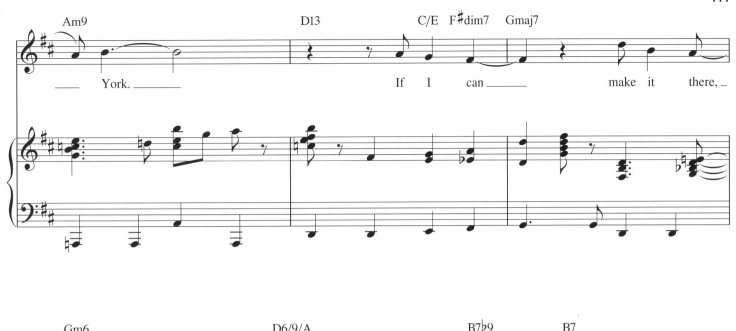

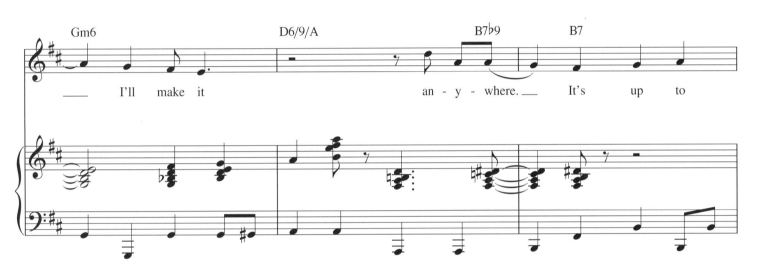

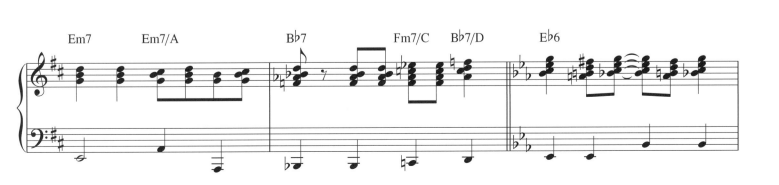

New York, _ New York. _ I want to

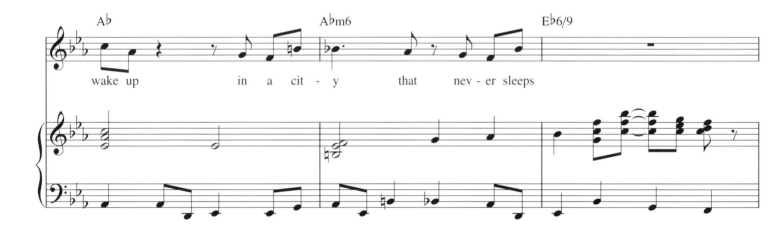

wake up in a cit - y that nev - er sleeps

and find I'm a - num - ber one, _ top of the list,

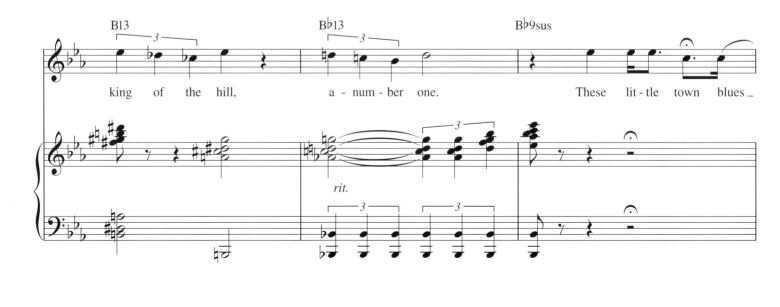

king of the hill, a - num - ber one. These lit - tle town blues _

Slowly

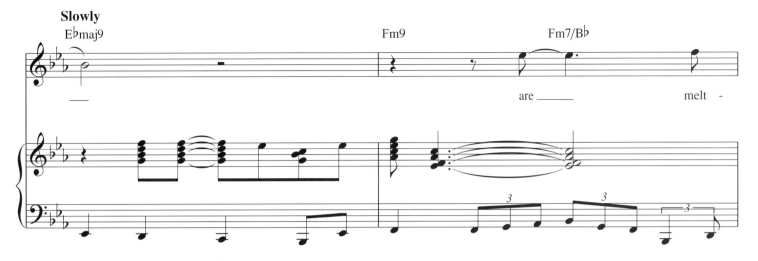

are _____ melt -

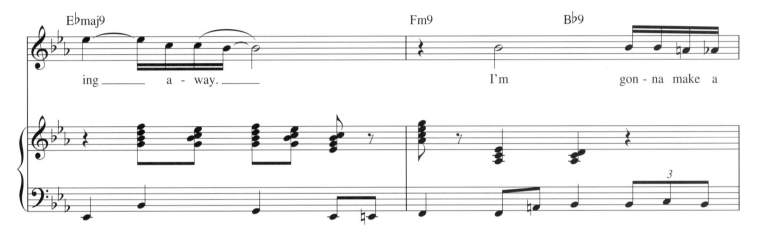

ing _____ a - way. _____ I'm gon - na make a

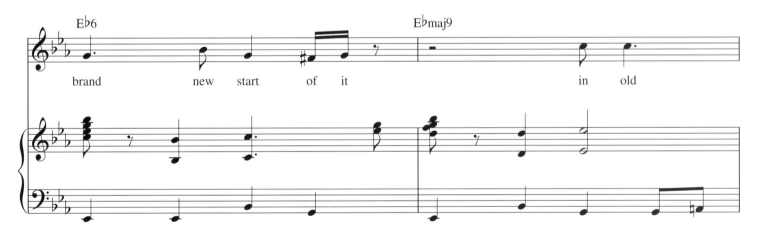

brand new start of it in old

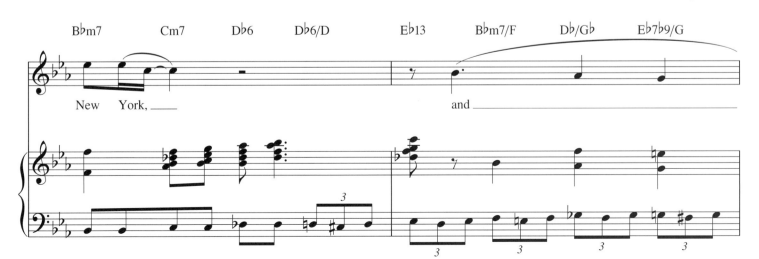

New York, _____ and _____

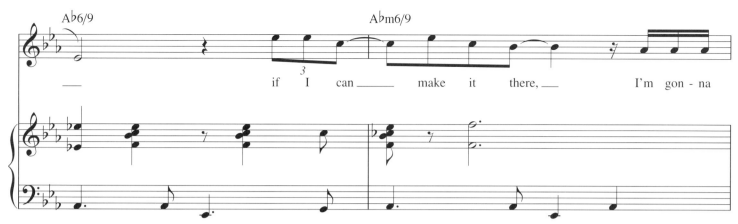

if I can ___ make it there, ___ I'm gon - na

Faster

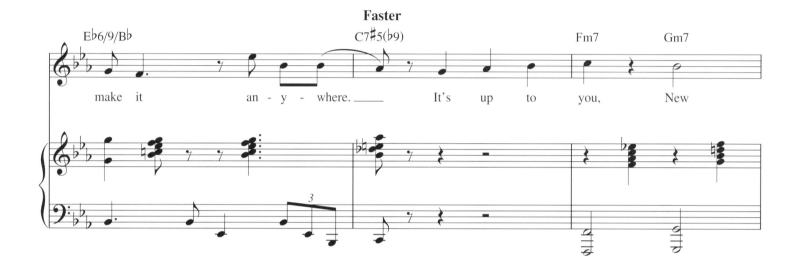

make it an - y - where. ___ It's up to you, New

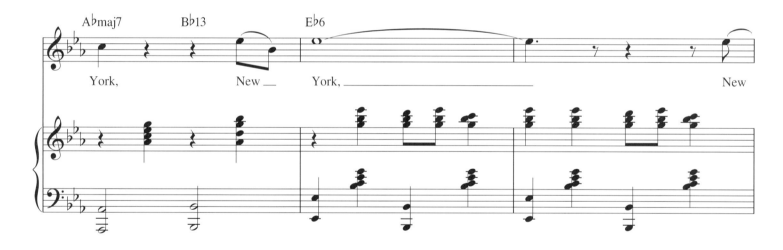

York, New ___ York, ___ New

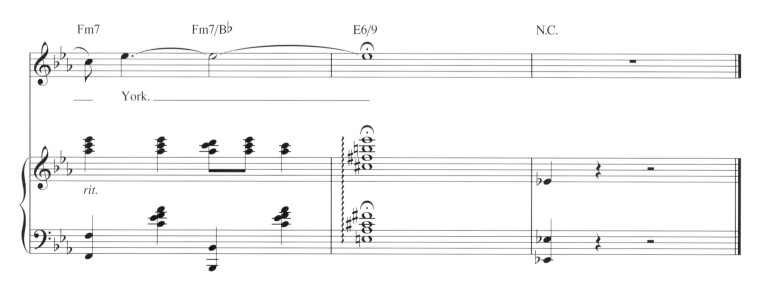

York. ___

PICK YOURSELF UP

Words by DOROTHY FIELDS
Music by JEROME KERN

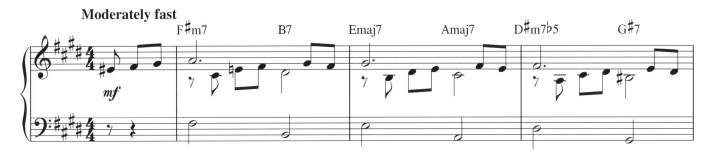

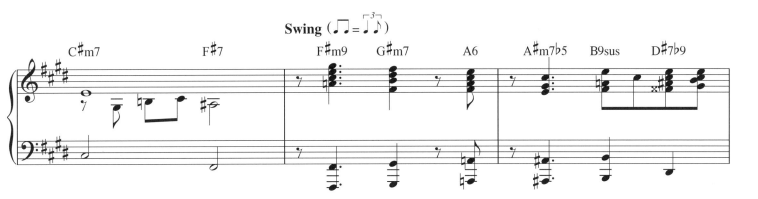

Now _____ noth - ing's im - pos - si - ble,

I have found, for when my chin is on _____ the ground: _ I pick _

Copyright © 1936 UNIVERSAL - POLYGRAM INTERNATIONAL PUBLISHING, INC. and ALDI MUSIC
Copyright Renewed
Print Rights for ALDI MUSIC in the U.S. Controlled and Administered by HAPPY ASPEN MUSIC LLC c/o SHAPIRO, BERNSTEIN & CO., INC.
All Rights Reserved   Used by Permission

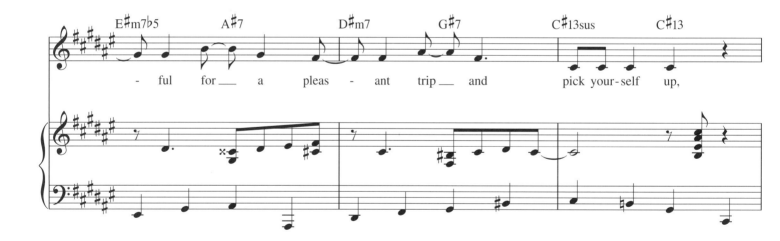

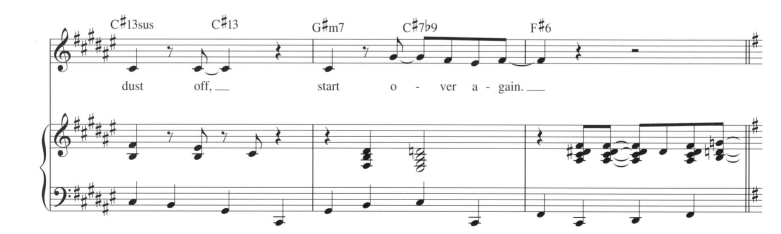

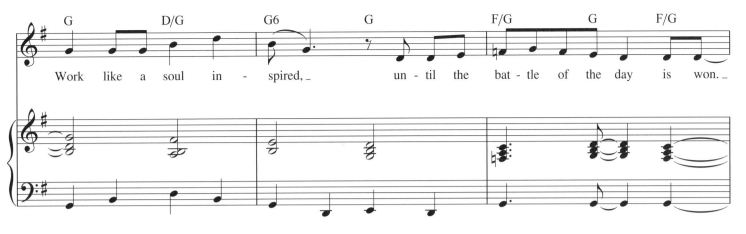

Work like a soul in-spired, ___ un-til the bat-tle of the day is won. ___

___ You may be sick and tired, ___ but you'll

be a man, ___ my son. Will you re-mem-ber the fa-

- mous men who had to fall ___ to rise ___ a - gain? ___ So

take a deep breath, pick your-self up, start all o-ver a-gain.

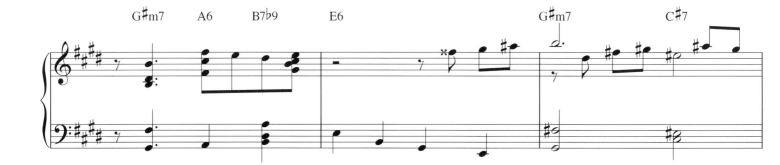

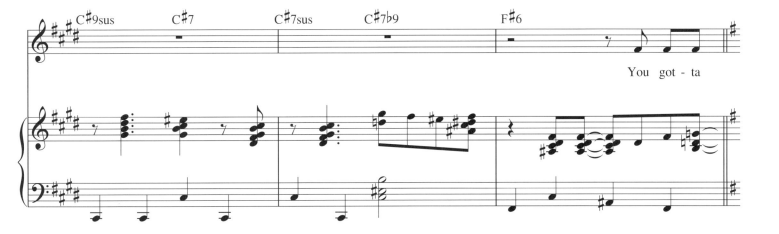

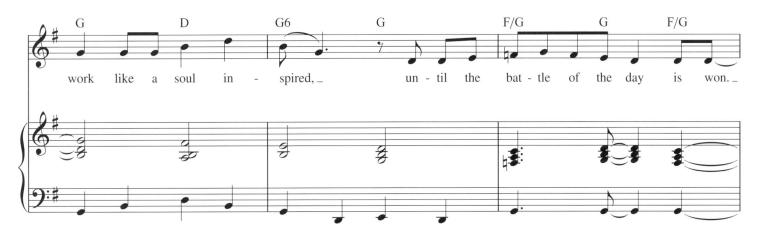

be a man,___ my son.

Will you re-mem-ber the

fa-mous men___ who had to fall___ and then rise a-gain?___ So

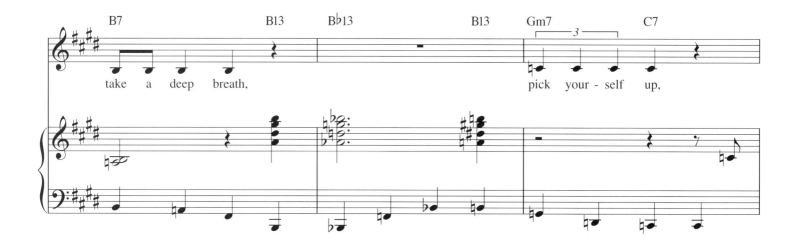

take a deep breath,

pick your-self up,

dust___ your-self off,

and

start all o-ver a-gain.

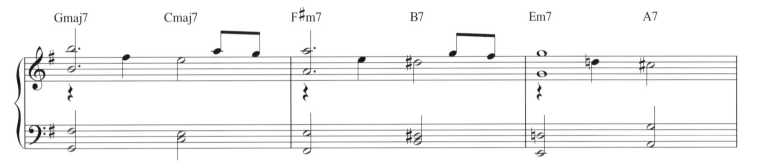

Once a-gain now!

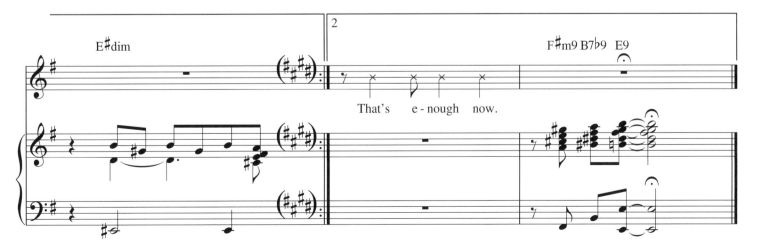

That's e-nough now.

NICE 'N' EASY

Words and Music by LEW SPENCE,
ALAN BERGMAN and MARILYN BERGMAN

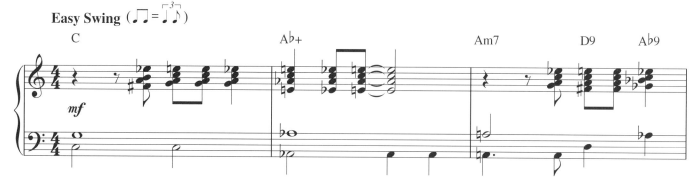

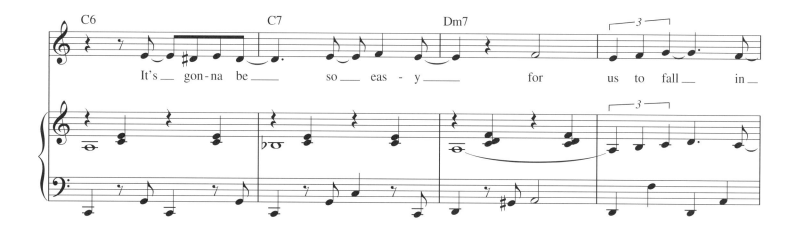

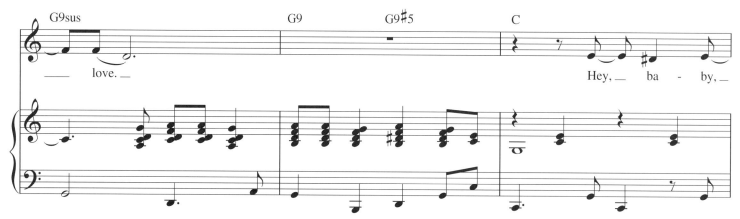

Copyright © 1960 Lew Spence Music and Spirit Catalog Holdings, S.a.r.l.
Copyright Renewed
All Rights for Lew Spence Music Controlled and Administered in the U.S. and Canada by Spirit Two Music, Inc.
All Rights for Spirit Catalog Holdings, S.a.r.l. Controlled and Administered by Spirit Two Music, Inc.
International Copyright Secured   All Rights Reserved

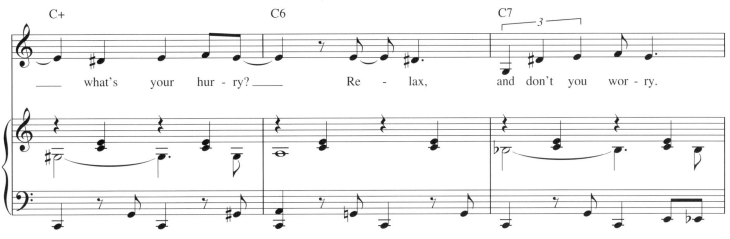

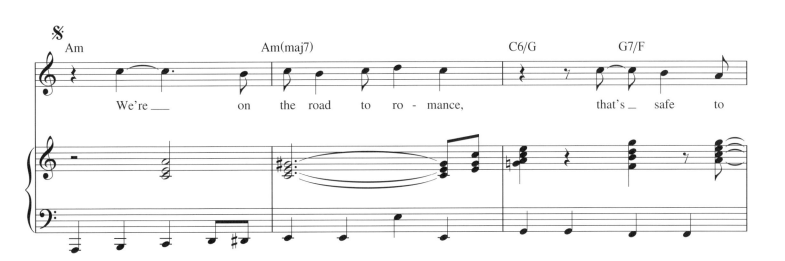

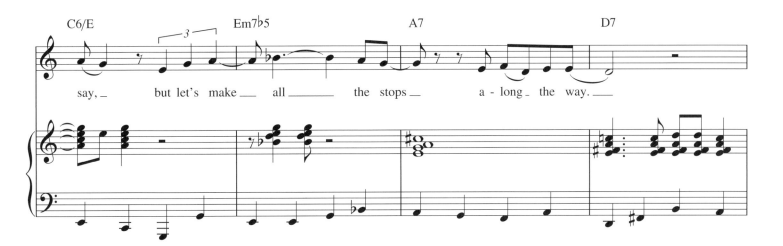

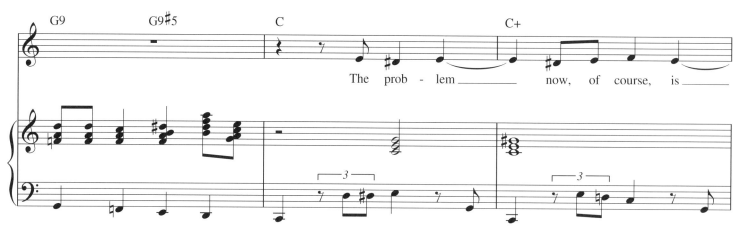

The prob - lem _____ now, of course, is _____

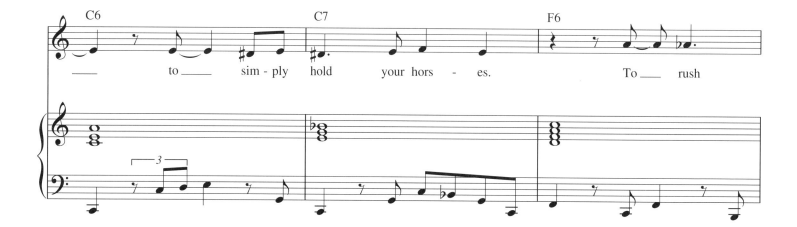

_____ to _____ sim - ply hold your hors - es. To _____ rush

would be _____ a crime, _____ 'cause _____

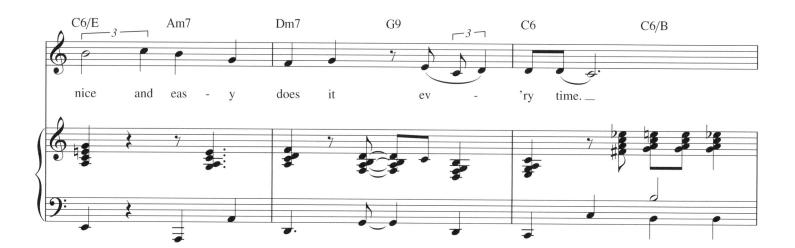

nice and eas - y does it ev - 'ry time. _____

D.S. al Coda

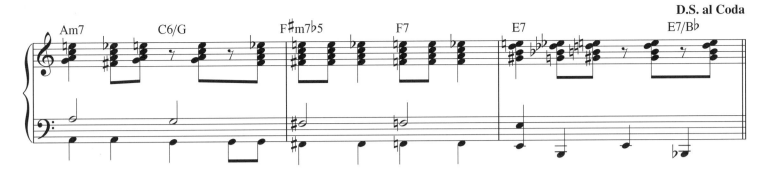

CODA

nice   and eas - y   does it,   nice   and eas - y
Nice   and eas - y   does it,

does   it,   nice   and eas - y   does it   ev - 'ry

time.   (Like the man   says, "One more   time.")   time.

ONE FOR MY BABY
(And One More for the Road)

Lyric by JOHNNY MERCER
Music by HAROLD ARLEN

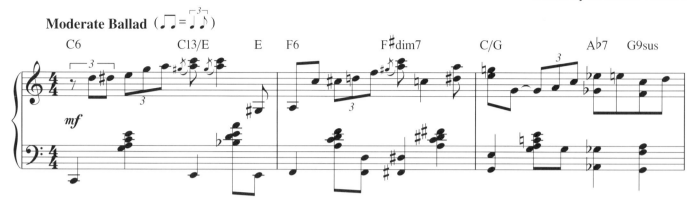

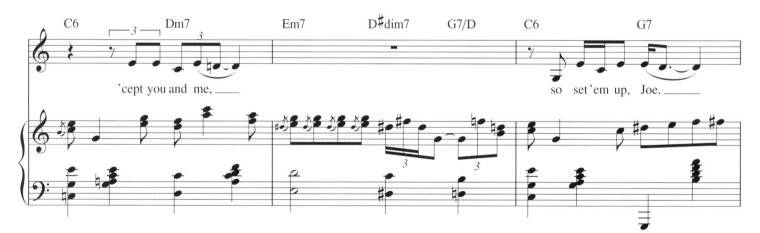

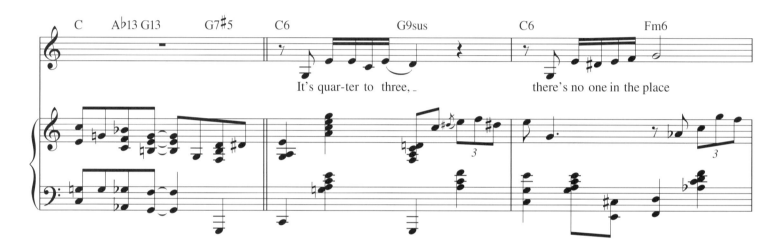

© 1943 (Renewed) HARWIN MUSIC CO.
All Rights Reserved

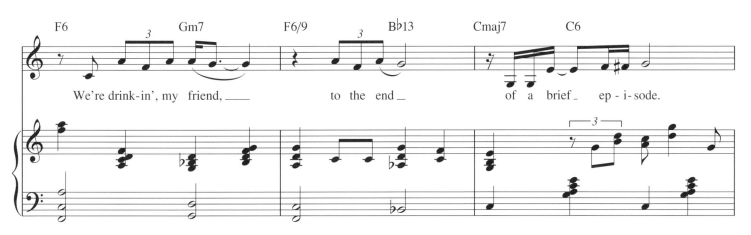

We're drink-in', my friend, ____ to the end ____ of a brief ____ ep - i - sode.

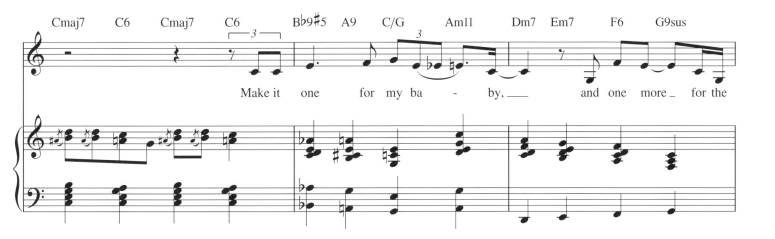

Make it one for my ba - by, ____ and one more ____ for the

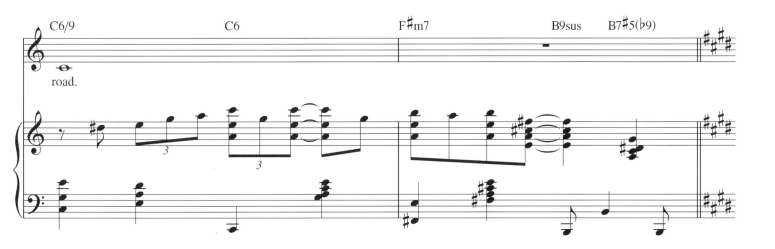

road.

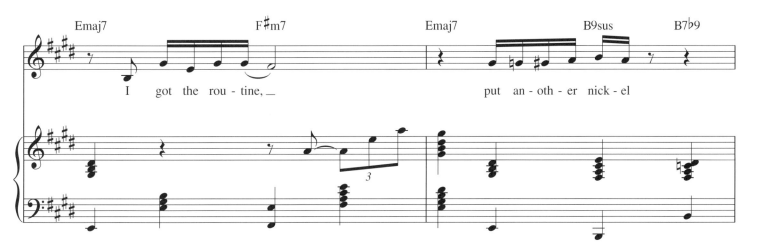

I got the rou - tine, ____ put an - oth - er nick - el

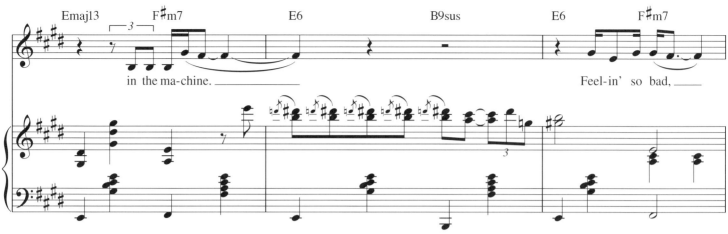

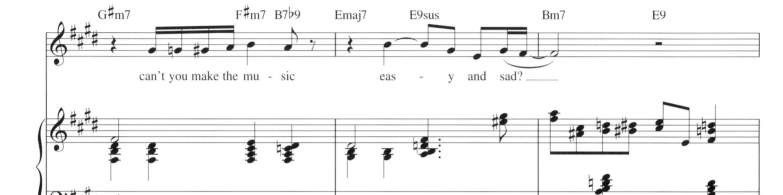

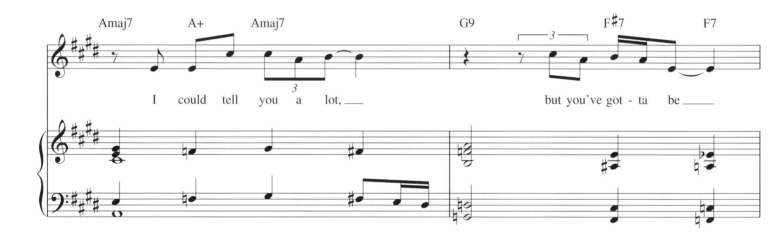

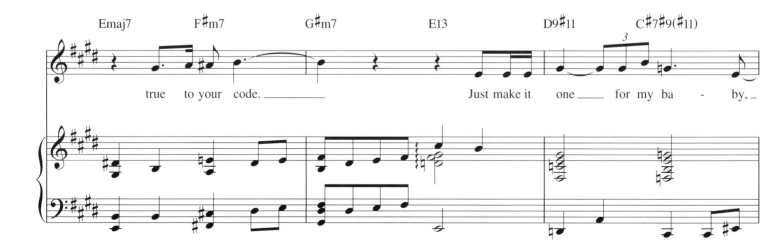

and one more ___ for the road. _____

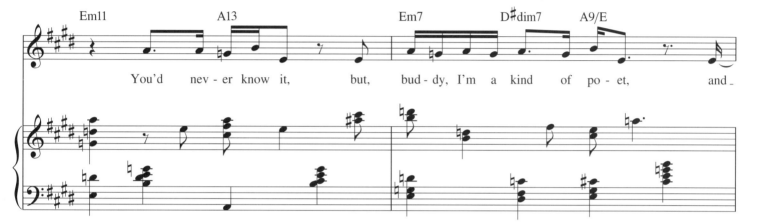

You'd nev-er know it, but, bud-dy, I'm a kind of po-et, and _

__ I've got a lot of things I'd like to say, _

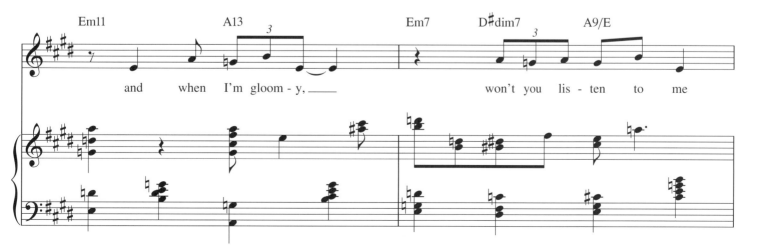

and when I'm gloom-y, ___ won't you lis-ten to me

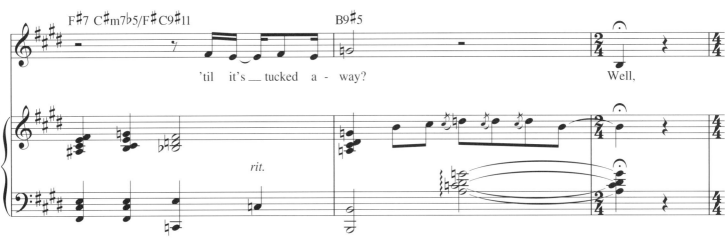

'til it's __ tucked a-way?   Well,

rit.

that's how it goes, __   and Joe, I know you're get-tin' __   anx-ious to close, __

a tempo

__ and thanks for the cheer. __   I hope you did-n't mind __

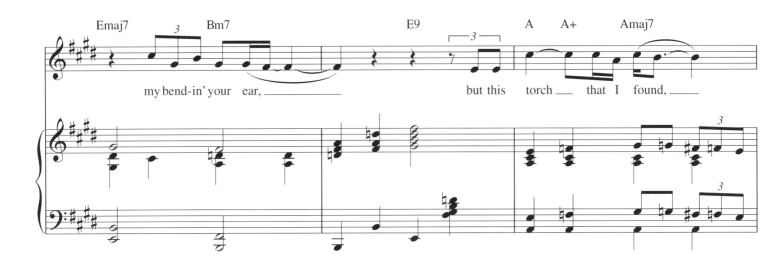

my bend-in' your ear, __   but this torch __ that I found, __

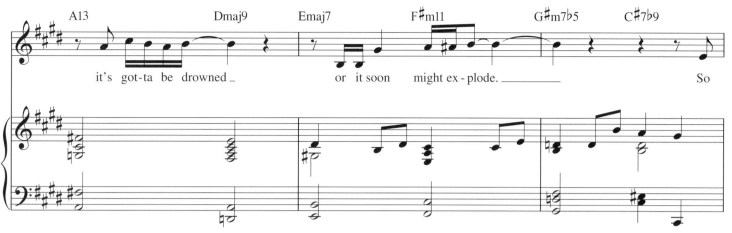

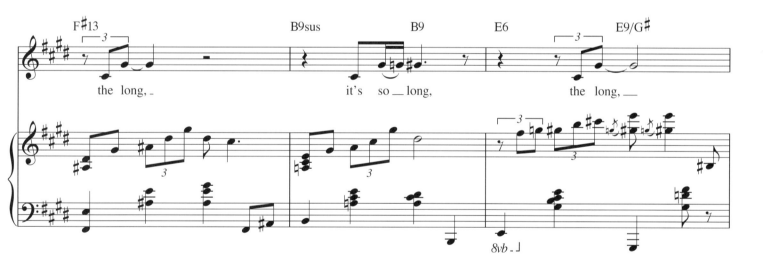

SATURDAY NIGHT
(Is the Loneliest Night of the Week)

Words by SAMMY CAHN
Music by JULE STYNE

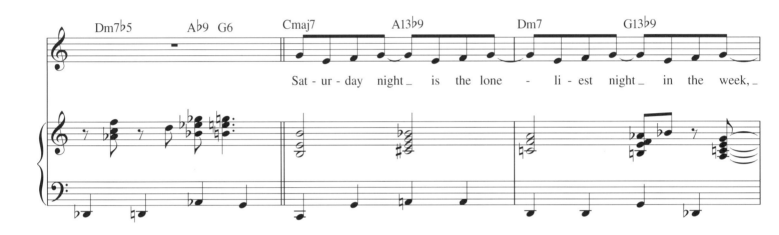

Sat - ur - day night _ is the lone - li - est night _ in the week,

_ 'cause _ that's the night that my sweet - ie and I _

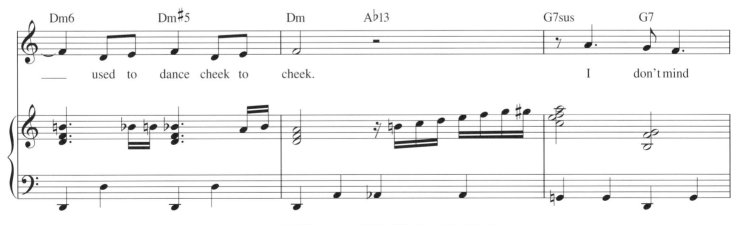

_ used to dance cheek to cheek. I don't mind

Copyright © 1944 by Producers Music Publishing Co. and Cahn Music Co.
Copyright Renewed
All Rights for Producers Music Publishing Co. Administered by Chappell & Co.
All Rights for Cahn Music Co. Administered by WB Music Corp.
International Copyright Secured   All Rights Reserved

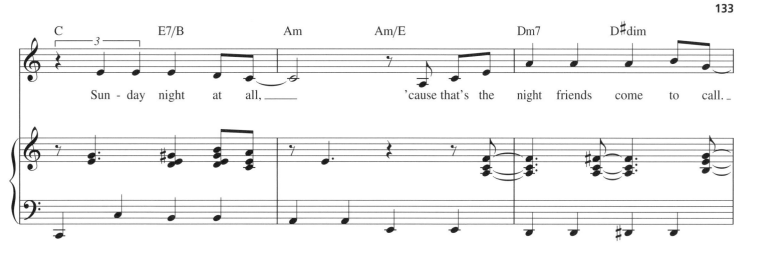

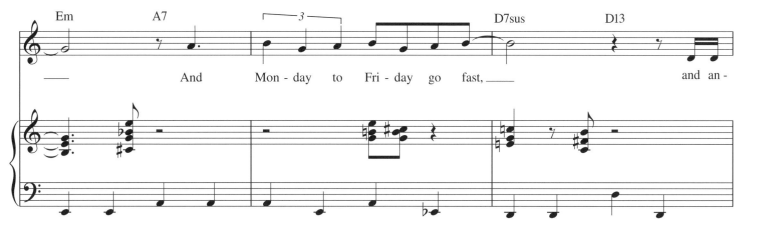

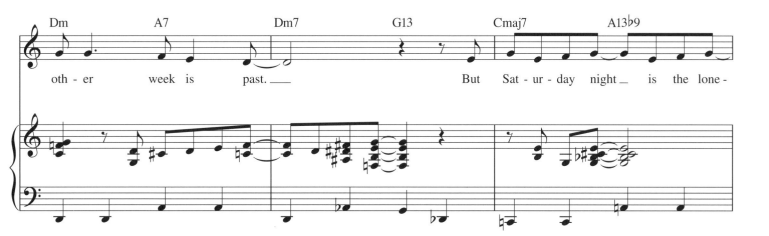

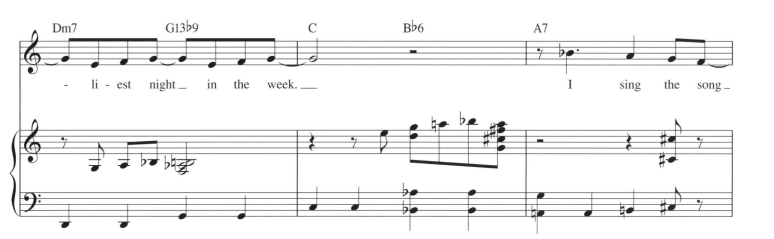

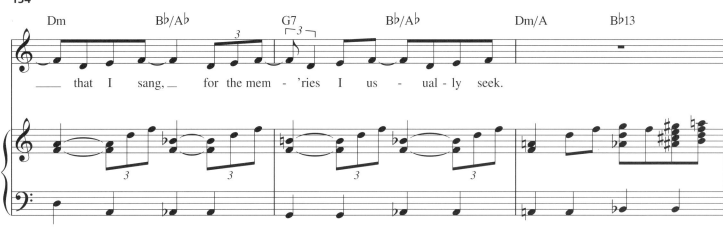

that I sang, __ for the mem - 'ries I us - ual-ly seek.

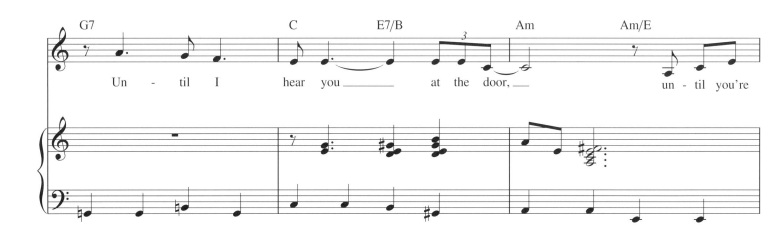

Un - til I hear you _____ at the door, __ un - til you're

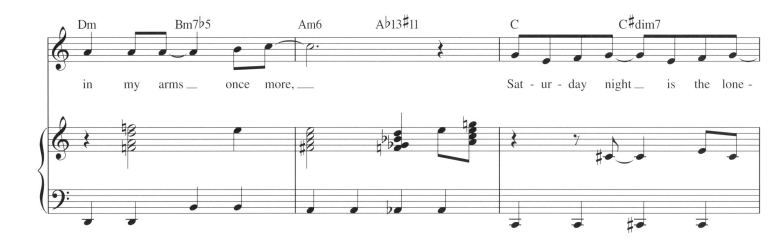

in my arms __ once more, __ Sat - ur - day night __ is the lone -

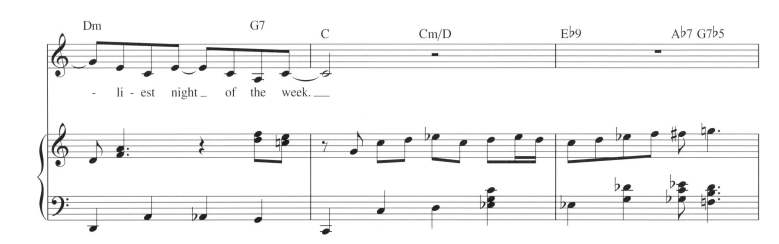

- li - est night __ of the week. __

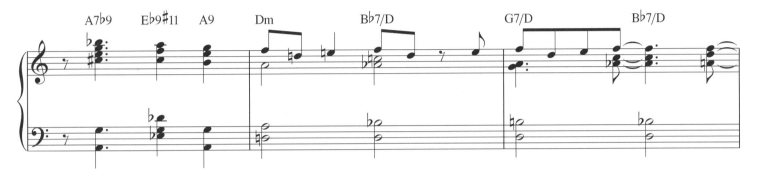

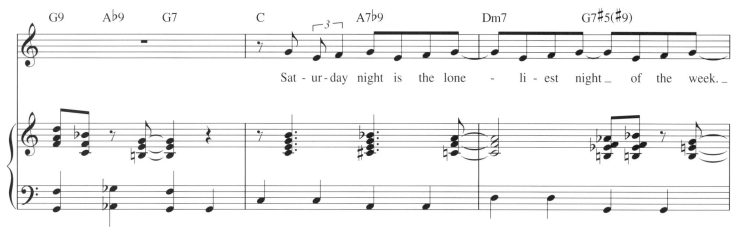

Sat - ur - day night is the lone - li - est night _ of the week. _

_ I sing the song _ that I sang _ for the mem -

'ries I us - ual - ly seek. _ Un - til I

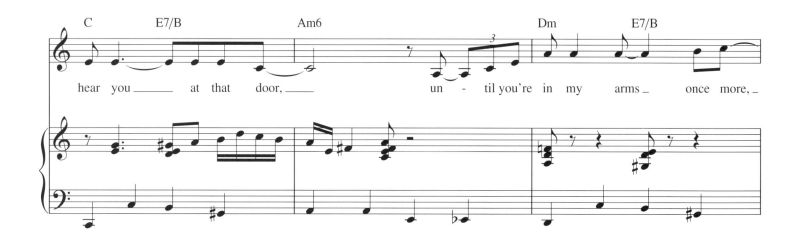

hear you _ at that door, _ un - til you're in my arms _ once more, _

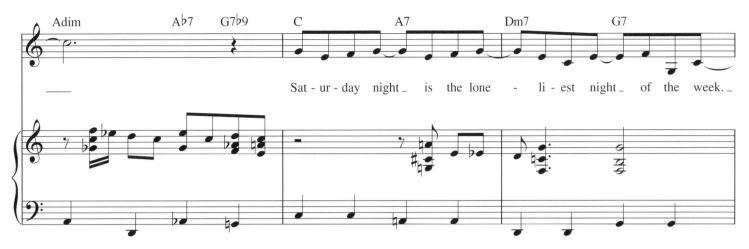

Sat - ur - day night _ is the lone - li - est night _ of the week. _

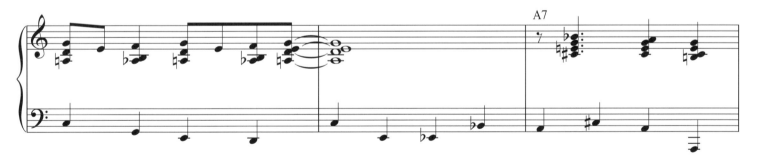

Un - til I hear ___ you ___ at the door, ___ un - til you're

in my arms ___ once more, ___

Sat - ur - day night ___ is the lone - li - est night ___ of the week. ___

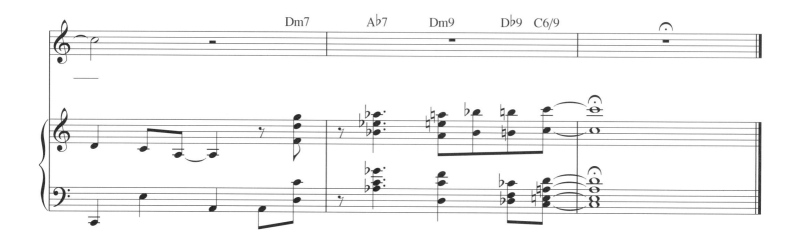

THE SEPTEMBER OF MY YEARS

Words by SAMMY CAHN
Music by JAMES VAN HEUSEN

Copyright © 1965 Cahn Music Co. and Van Heusen Music Corp.
Copyright Renewed
All Rights for Cahn Music Co. Administered by WB Music Corp.
International Copyright Secured   All Rights Reserved

Moderately slow Ballad

all? As a man who has al - ways had ____ the wan - d'ring ways, now I'm reach - ing back for yes - ter - days, 'til a long for - got - ten love ap - pears.

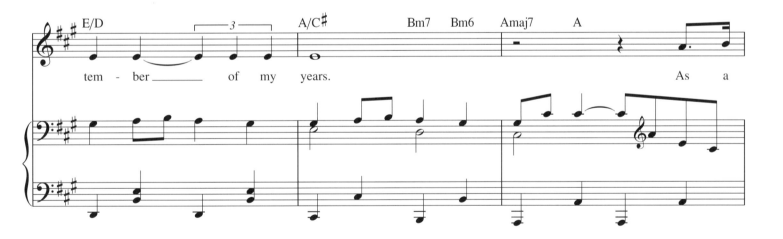

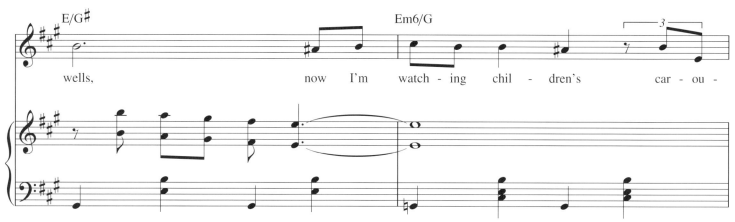

wells, now I'm watch - ing chil - dren's car - ou -

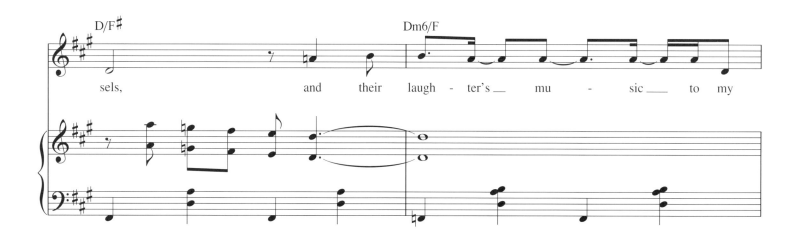

sels, and their laugh - ter's __ mu - sic __ to my

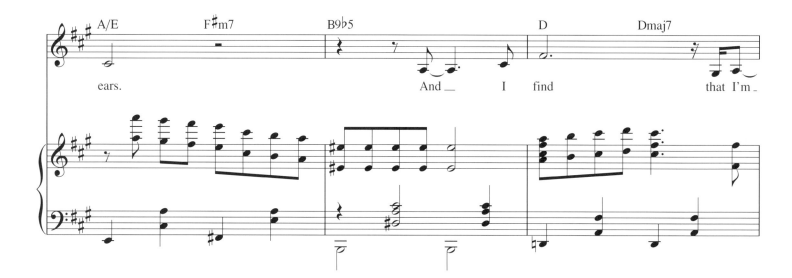

ears. And __ I find that I'm __

__ smil - ing gent - ly, as I near Sep - tem - ber, the

warm _____ Sep - tem - ber of my years,

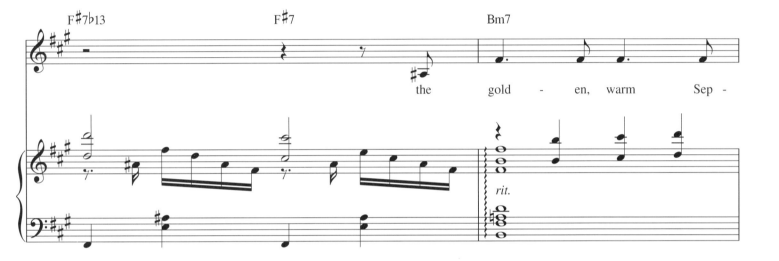

the gold - en, warm Sep -

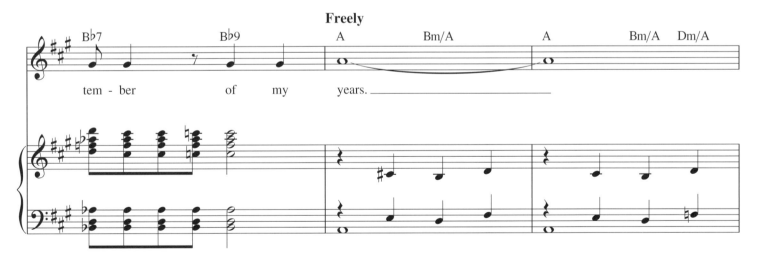

tem - ber of my years. _____

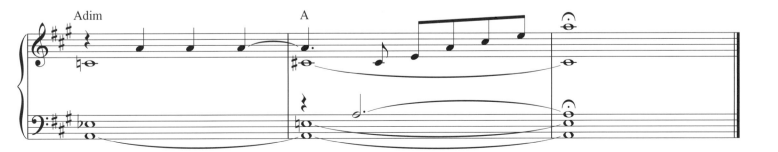

SUMMER WIND

English Words by JOHNNY MERCER
Original German Lyrics by HANS BRADTKE
Music by HENRY MAYER

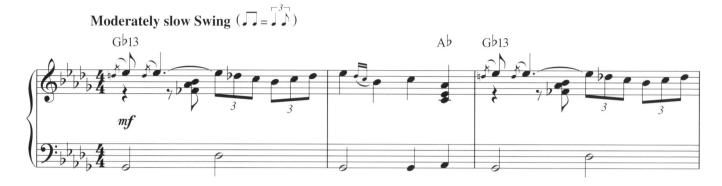

© 1965 (Renewed) THE JOHNNY MERCER FOUNDATION and EDITION PRIMUS ROLF BUDDE KG
All Rights Administered by WB MUSIC CORP.
All Rights Reserved   Used by Permission

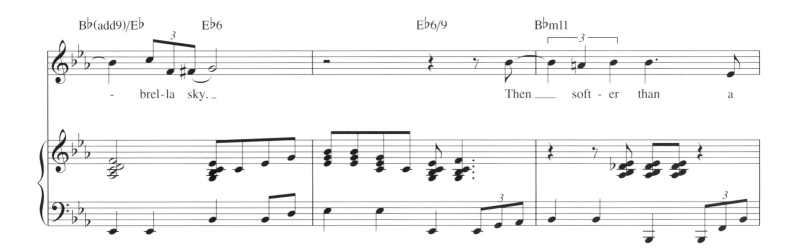

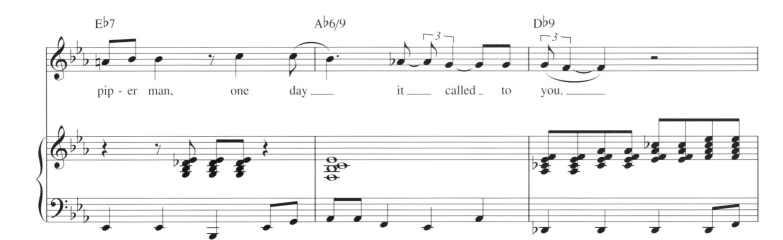

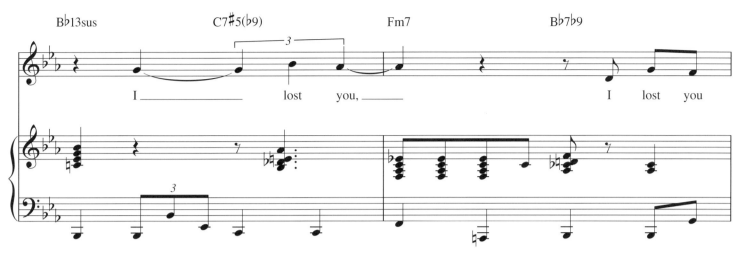

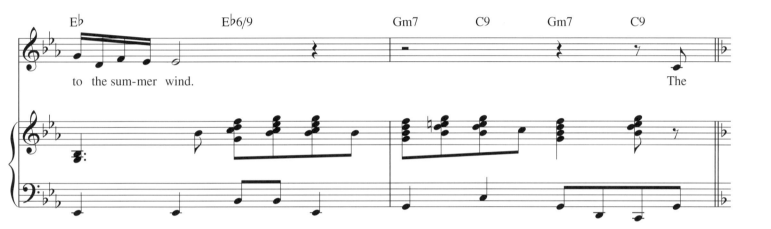

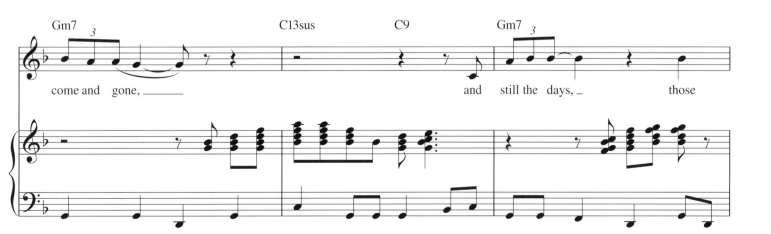

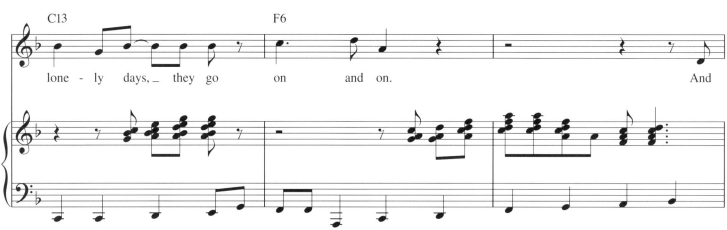

lone - ly days,_ they go on and on. And

guess who sighs _____ his _____ lull - a - bies _____ through

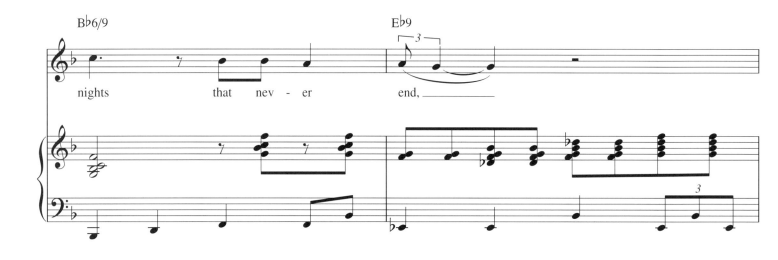

nights that nev - er end, _____

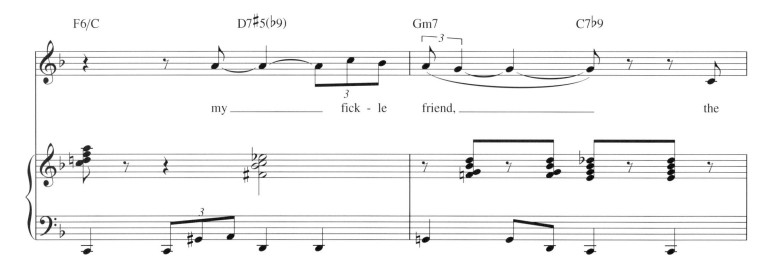

my _____ fick - le friend, _____ the

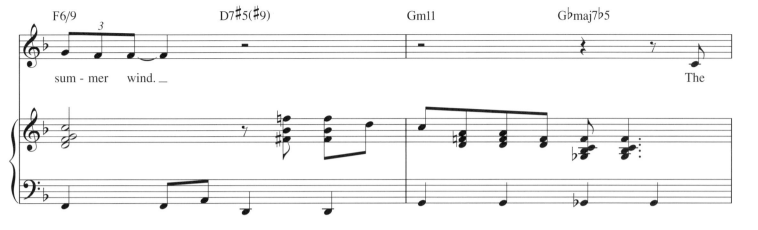

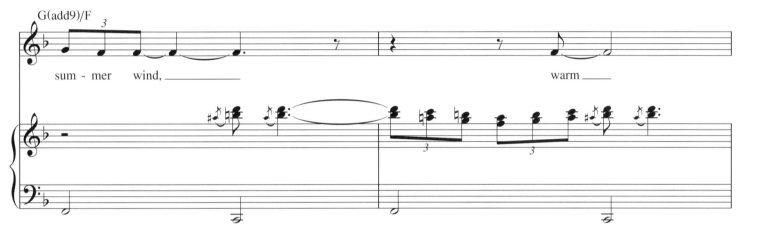

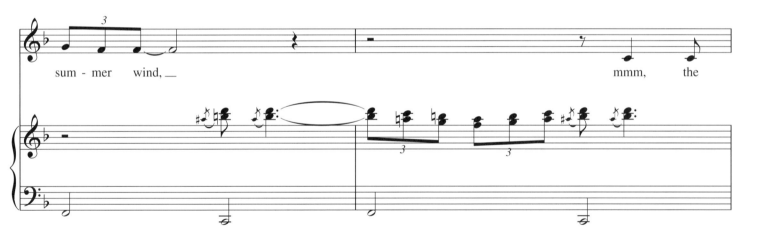

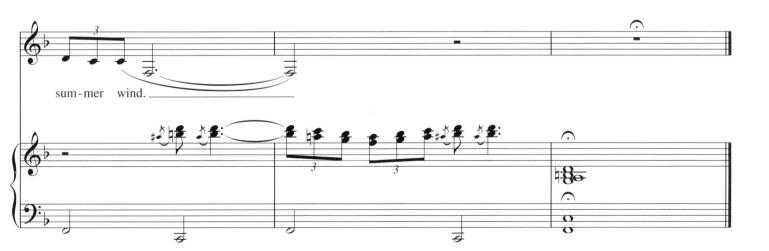

TEACH ME TONIGHT

Words by SAMMY CAHN
Music by GENE DePAUL

Copyright © 1953, 1954 Cahn Music Co. and Hub Music Company
Copyright Renewed
All Rights for Cahn Music Co. Administered by WB Music Corp.
International Copyright Secured   All Rights Reserved

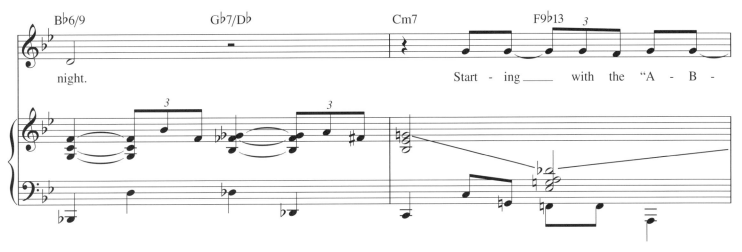

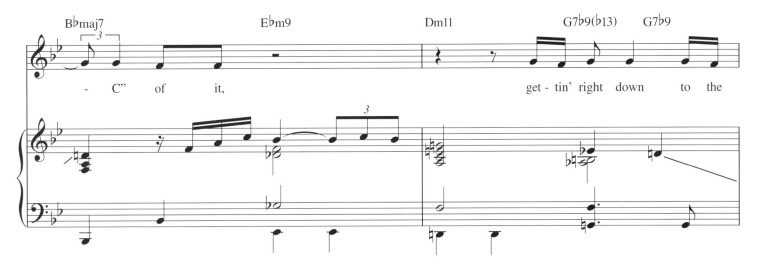

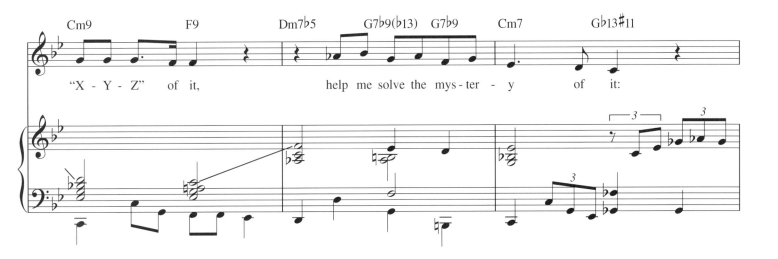

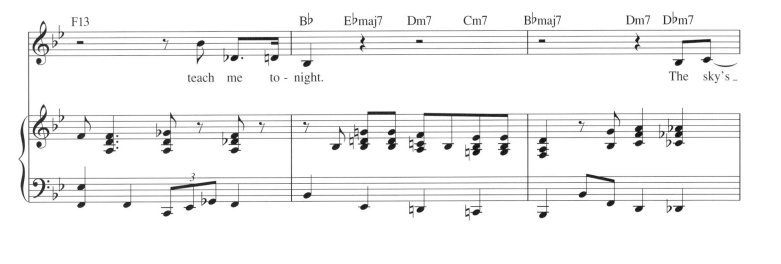

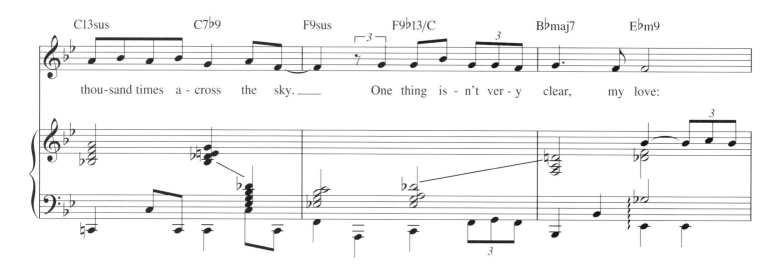

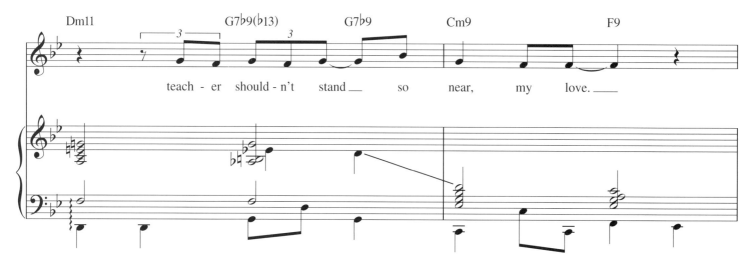

Grad-u-a-tion's al-most here, my love.

You'd bet-ter teach me to-night. ___

I've played love scenes ___ in a flick or two,

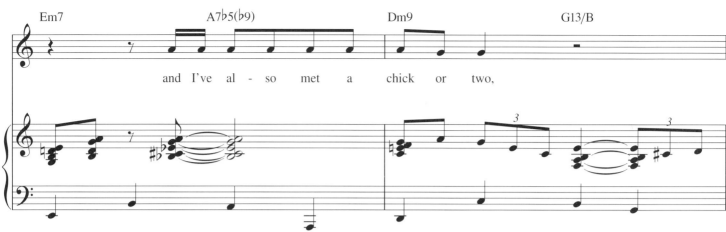

and I've al - so met a chick or two,

but I still can learn a _____ trick or two: _____ hey, _____ teach me to - night.

I, who thought I knew the

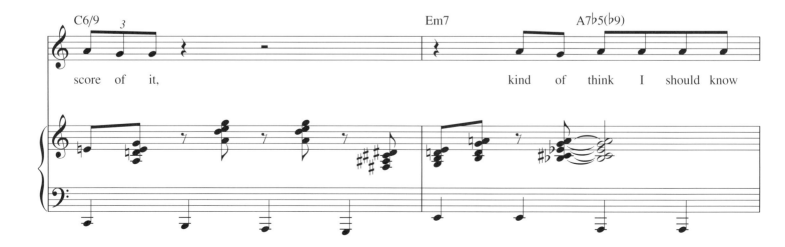

score of it, kind of think I should know

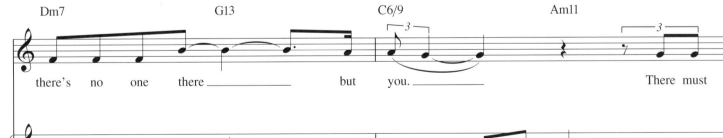

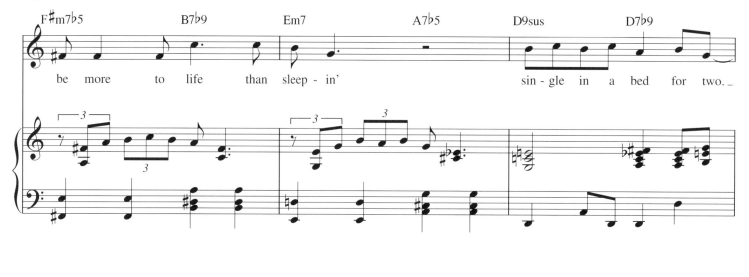

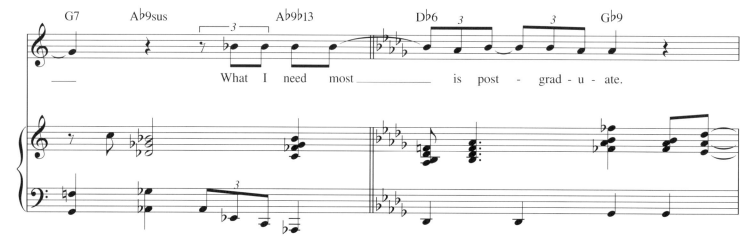

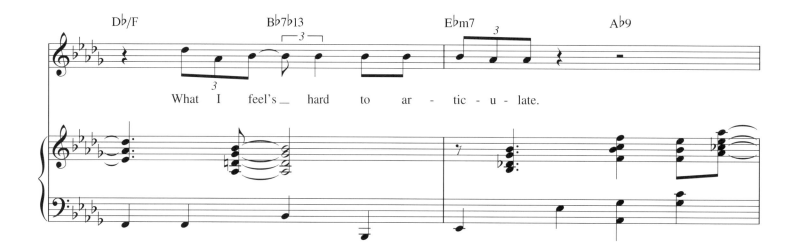

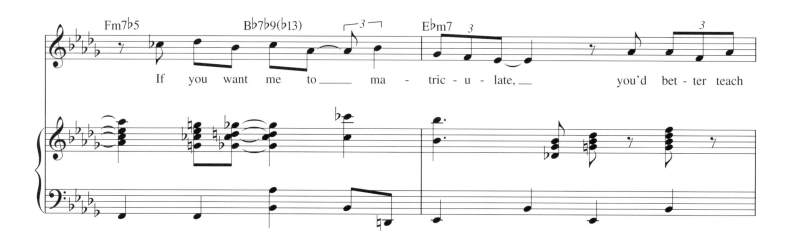

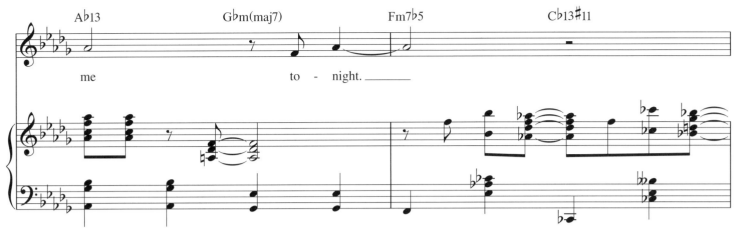

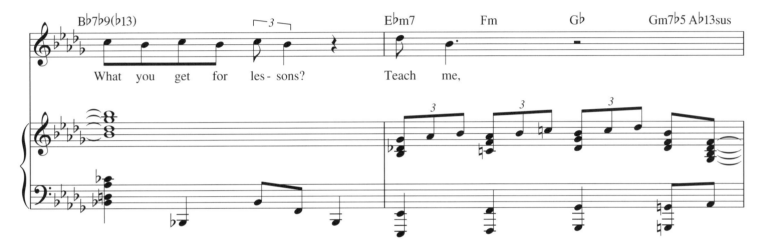

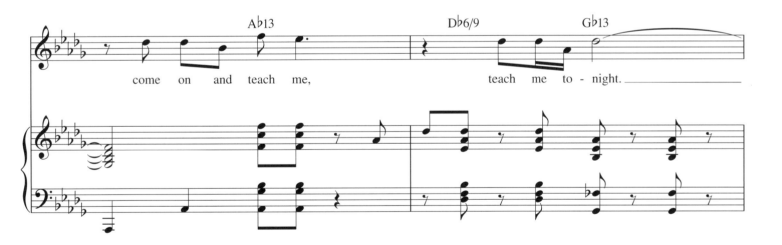

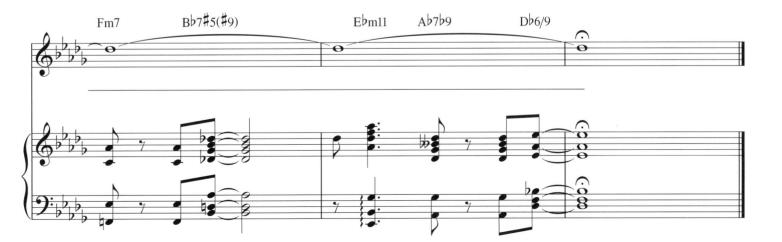

THAT'S LIFE

Words and Music by DEAN KAY
and KELLY GORDON

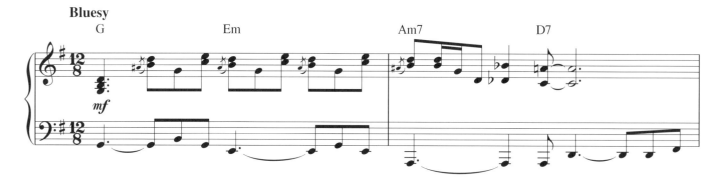

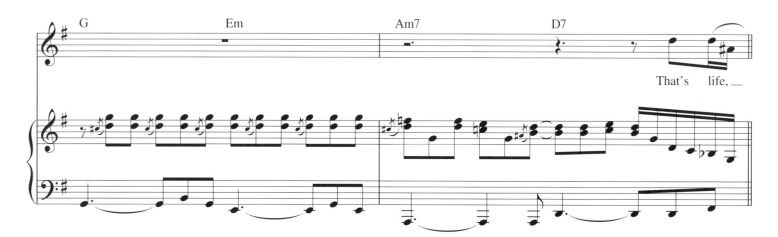

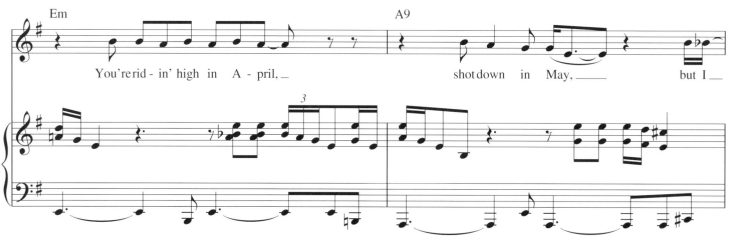

Copyright © 1964, 1966 UNIVERSAL - POLYGRAM INTERNATIONAL PUBLISHING, INC.
Copyright Renewed
All Rights Reserved   Used by Permission

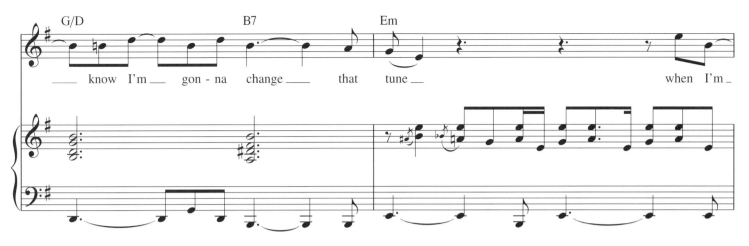

know I'm gon-na change that tune when I'm

back on top, back on top in June. I said that's life,

and as fun-ny as it may seem,

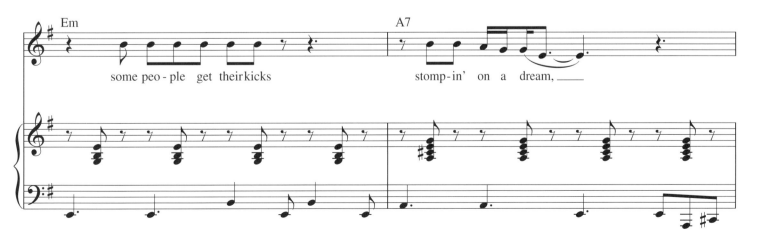

some peo-ple get their kicks stomp-in' on a dream,

but I don't let it, let it get me down, _____ 'cause this

fine old world, it keeps _ spin-nin' a - round. _____ I've been a

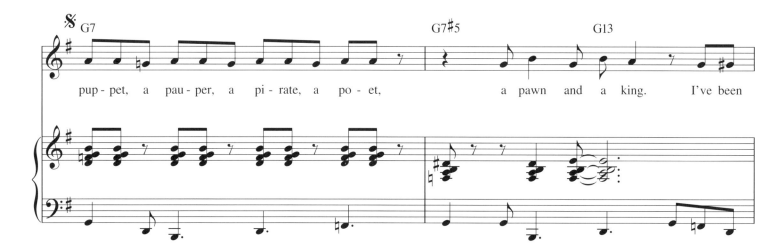

pup - pet, a pau - per, a pi - rate, a po - et, a pawn and a king. I've been

up and down and o - ver and out, and I know one thing, _ each time _

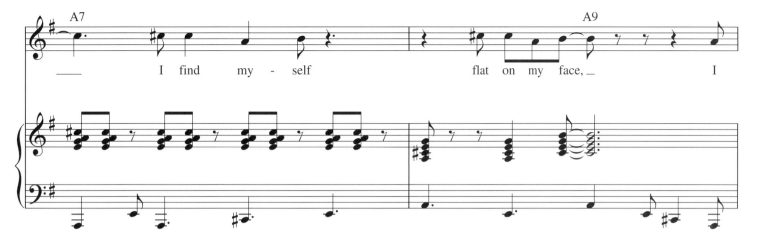

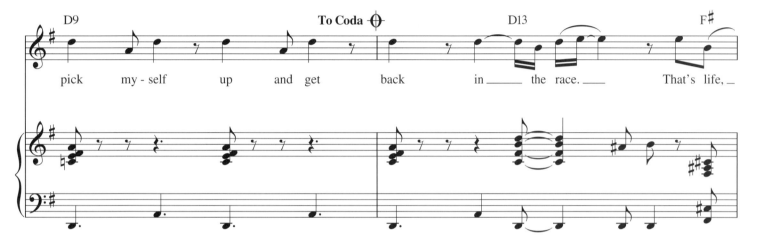

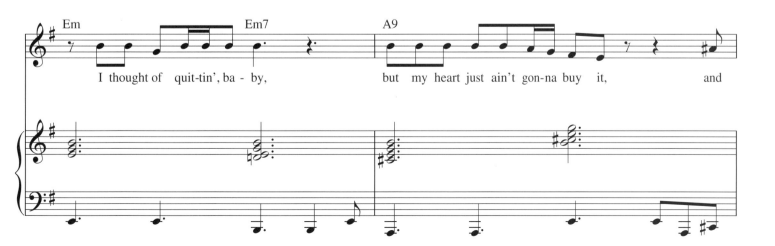

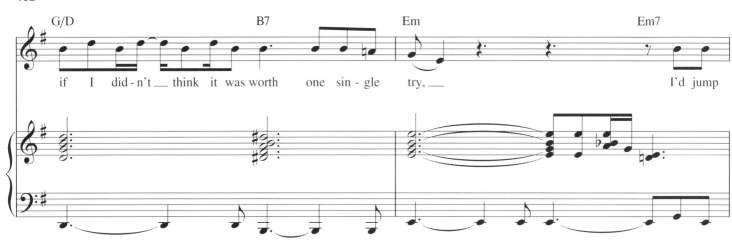

if I did-n't ___ think it was worth one sin-gle try, ___ I'd jump

right on a big ___ bird, ___ and then I'd fly. ___ I've been a

D.S. al Coda

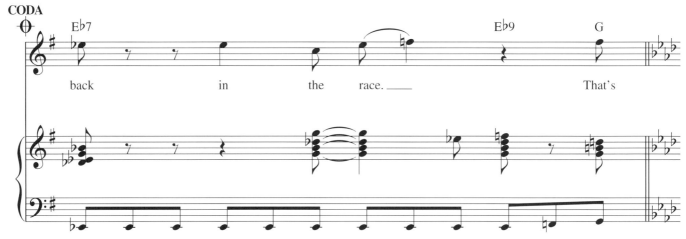

CODA

back in the race. ___ That's

life, ___ that's life, ___ and I can't ___ de-ny it.

Man - y times I thought of cut-tin' out, ___ but my heart won't buy it, but

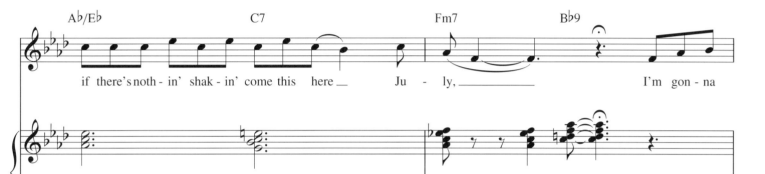

if there's noth - in' shak - in' come this here ___ Ju - ly, ___ I'm gon - na

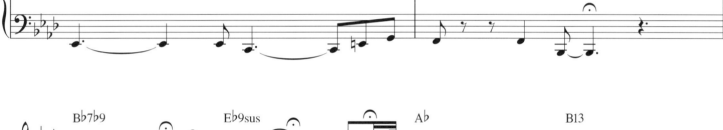

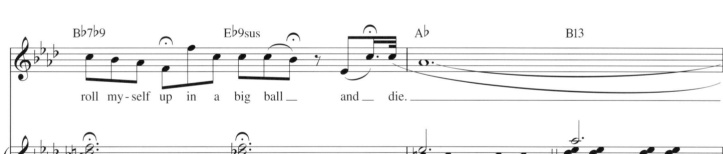

roll my-self up in a big ball ___ and ___ die. ___

My, my.

WAVE

Words and Music by
ANTONIO CARLOS JOBIM

Moderate Bossa Nova

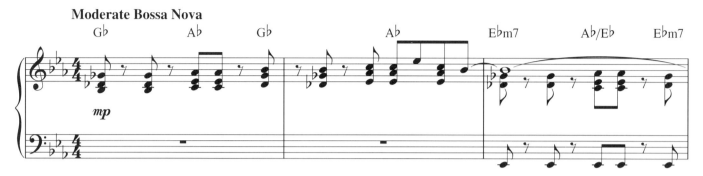

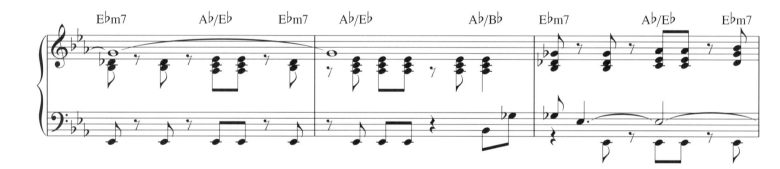

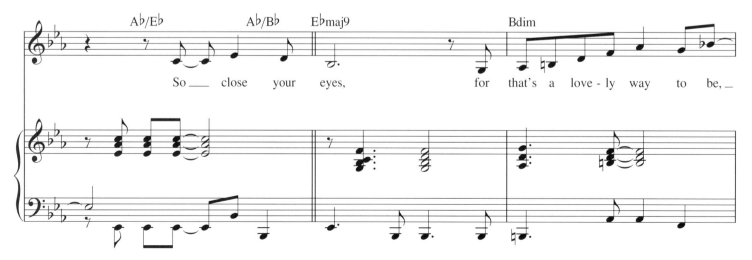

So ___ close your eyes, for that's a love-ly way to be, ___

Copyright © 1967, 1968 Antonio Carlos Jobim
Copyright Renewed
Published by Corcovado Music Corp.
International Copyright Secured   All Rights Reserved

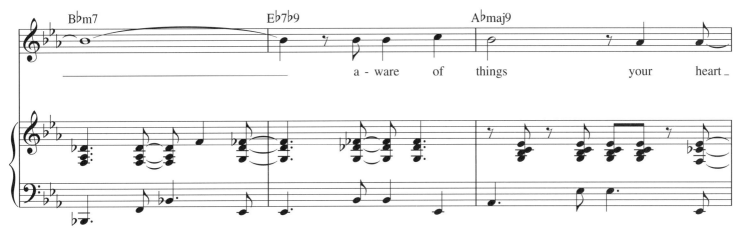

a - ware of things your heart

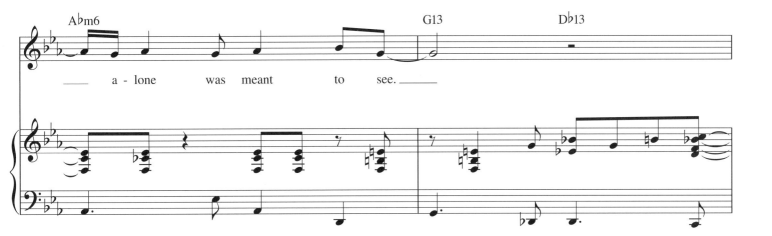

a - lone was meant to see.

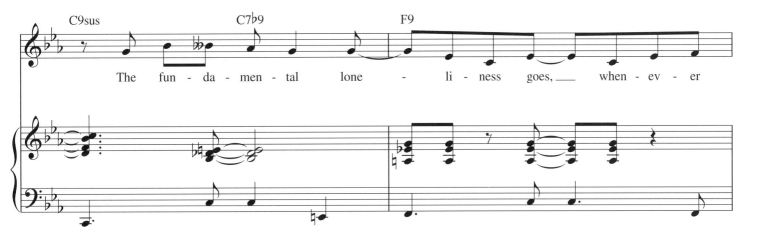

The fun - da - men - tal lone - li - ness goes, ___ when - ev - er

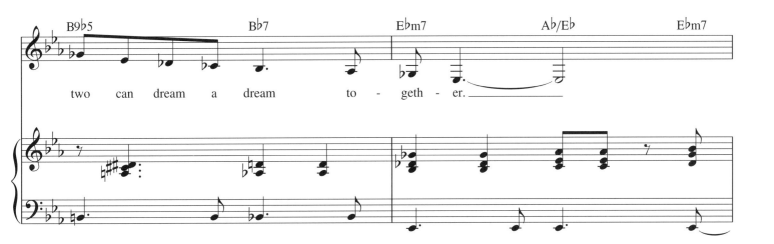

two can dream a dream to - geth - er. _____

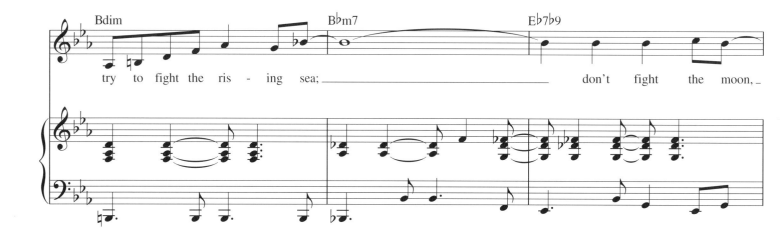

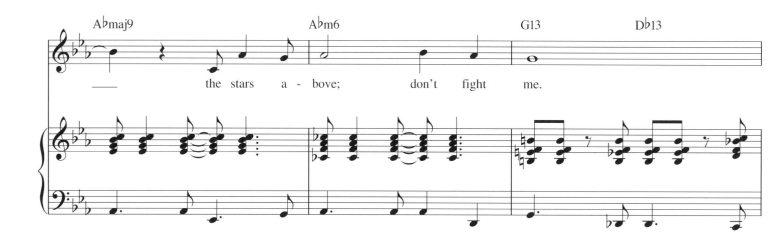

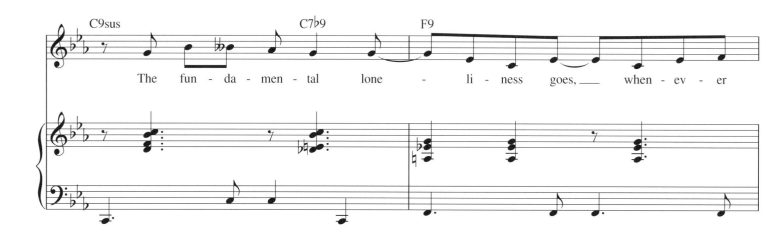

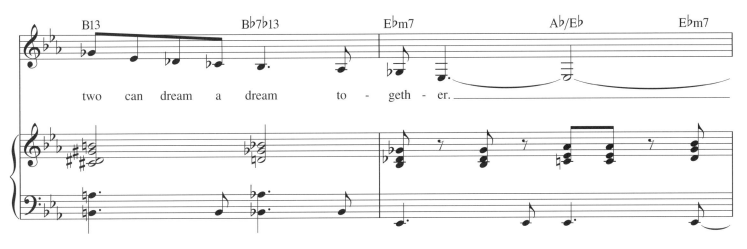

two can dream a dream to - geth - er. _____

When I saw you first, _____ the time was

half past three. When your

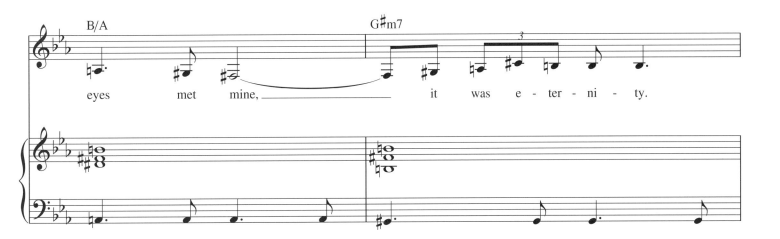

eyes met mine, _____ it was e - ter - ni - ty.

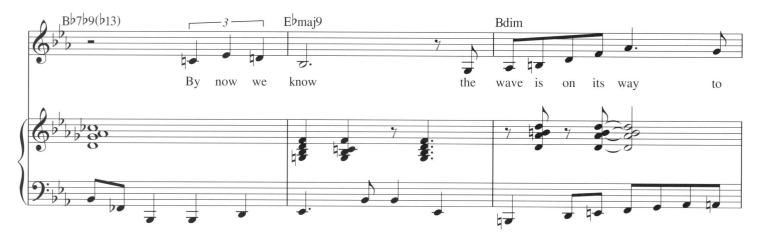

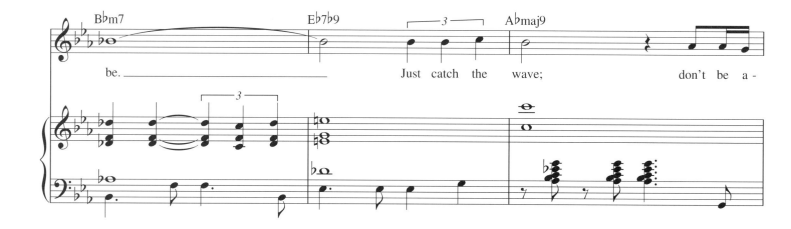

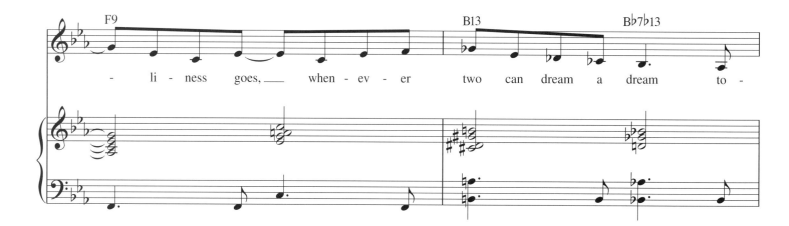

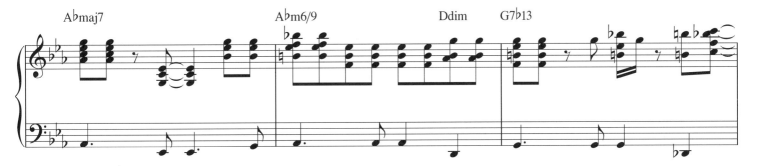

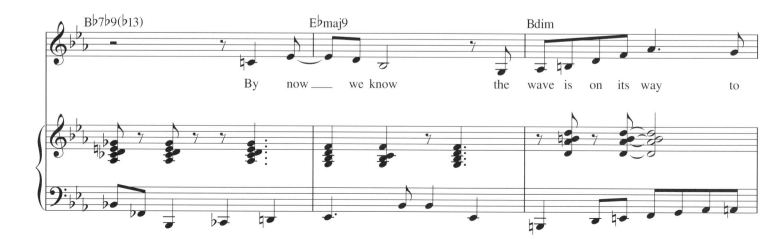

be. _____ Just catch that wave; don't be

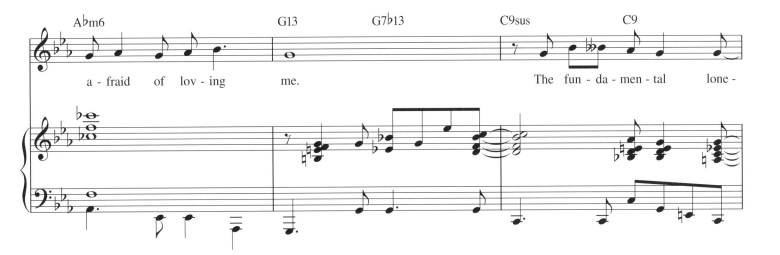

a - fraid of lov - ing me. The fun - da - men - tal lone -

- li - ness goes _ when-ev - er two can dream a dream to - geth - er. ____

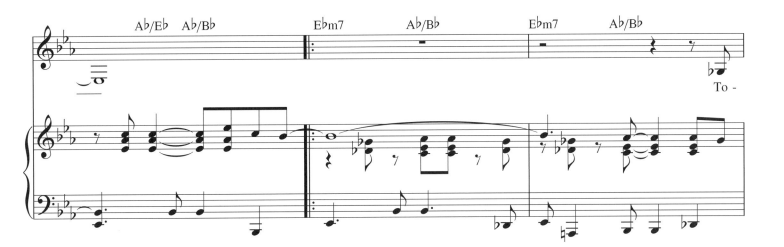

To -

geth - er.

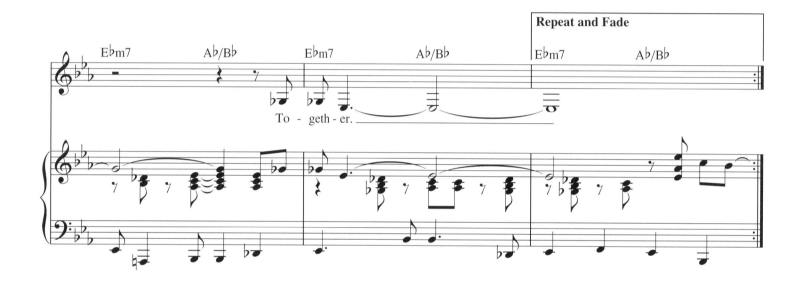

Repeat and Fade

To - geth - er.

Optional Ending

rit.

WITCHCRAFT

Music by CY COLEMAN
Lyrics by CAROLYN LEIGH

© 1957 MORLEY MUSIC CO.
Copyright Renewed and Assigned to MORLEY MUSIC CO. and NOTABLE MUSIC COMPANY, INC.
All Rights Reserved   Used by Permission

And I've got no de-fense___ for it, the heat is

too in-tense___ for it. What good would___ com-mon sense for it

do? 'Cause it's witch - craft,_____

___ wick-ed witch-craft,_____ and al-

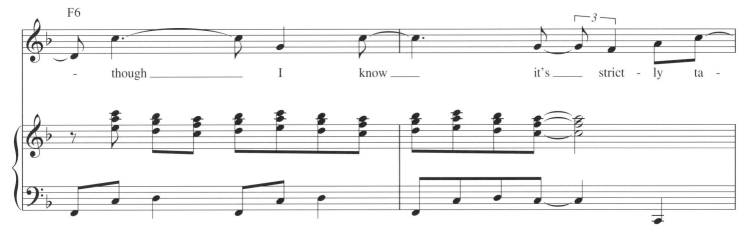

though _____ I know _____ it's _____ strict-ly ta-

-boo, _____ when you a-

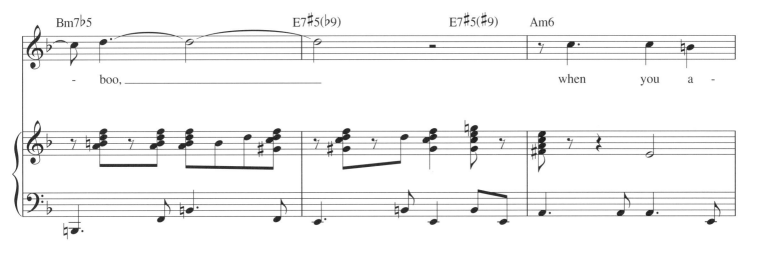

rouse the need ___ in me, my heart ___ says _____ yes, in-deed, in me.

Pro-ceed with what you're lead-ing me to.

It's ___ such an an-cient pitch, ___

To Coda ⊕

but one I would-n't switch, ___ 'cause there's no ___

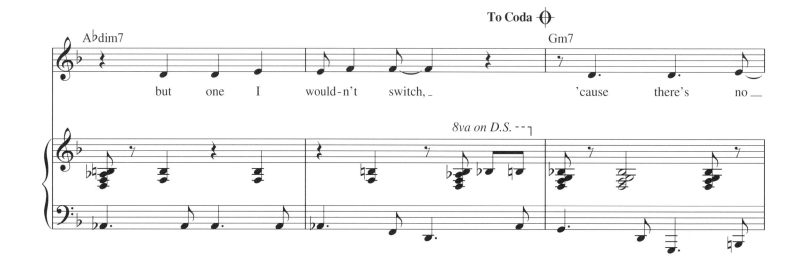

___ nic - er ___ witch than ___ you. ___

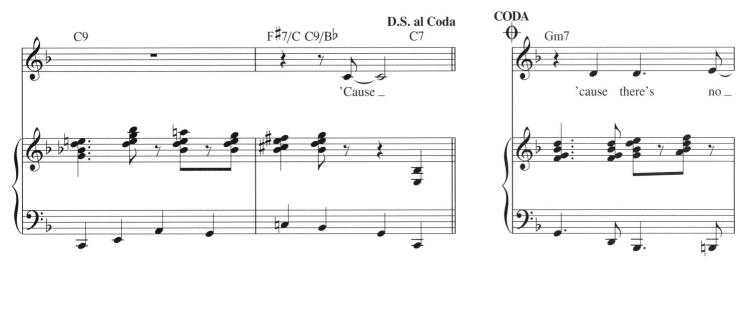

YOU MAKE ME FEEL SO YOUNG

Words by MACK GORDON
Music by JOSEF MYROW

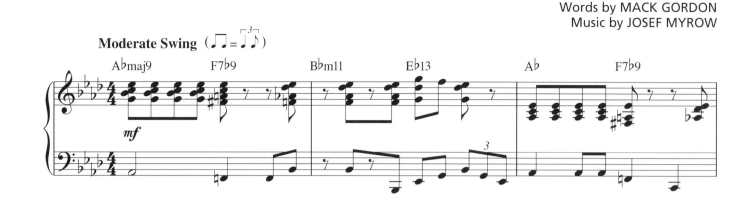

You make me feel so young, — you make me feel so "spring has sprung," — and ev'ry time — I —

— see you grin I'm such a hap-py in-di-vid-u-al.

© 1946 (Renewed) WB MUSIC CORP.
All Rights Reserved   Used by Permission

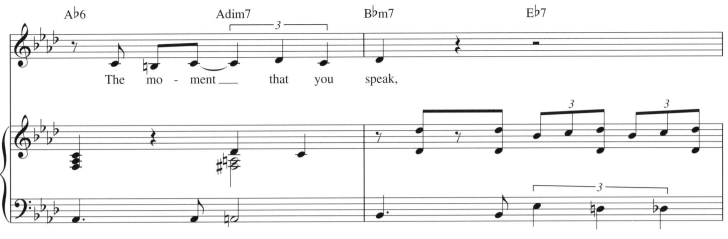

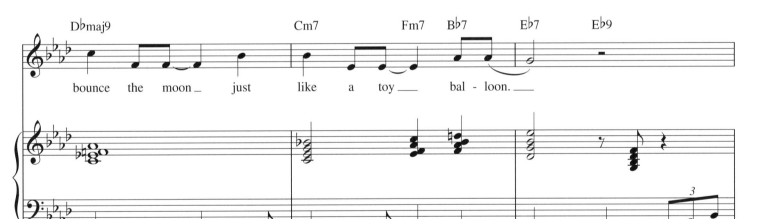

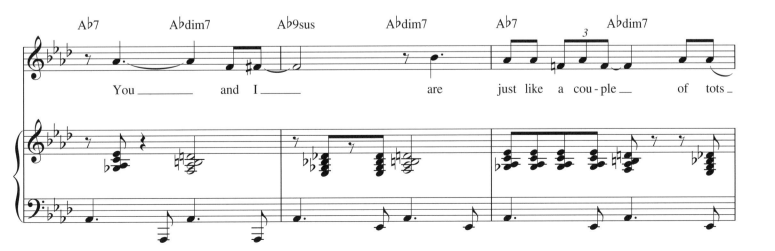

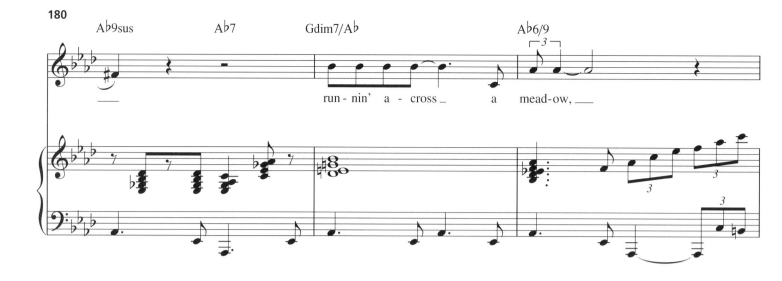

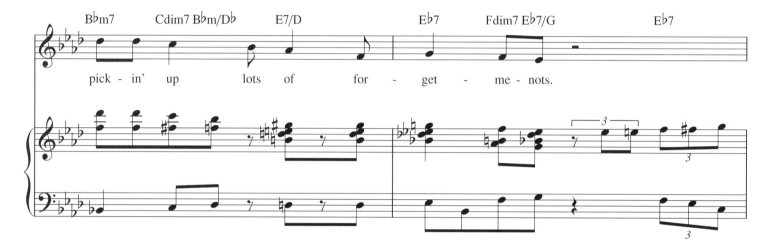

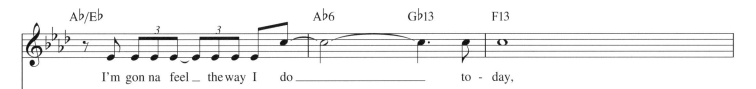

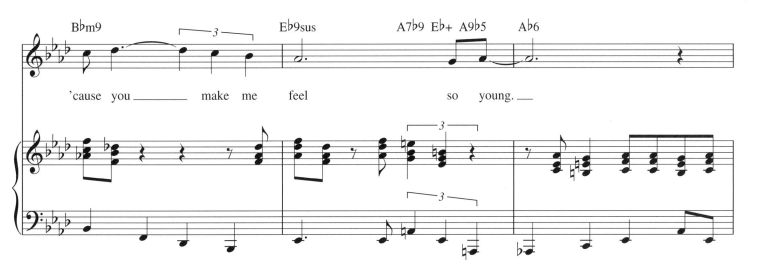

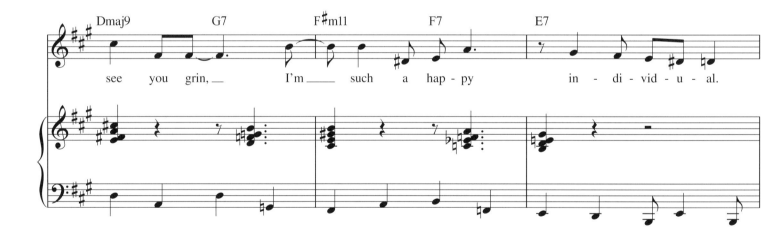

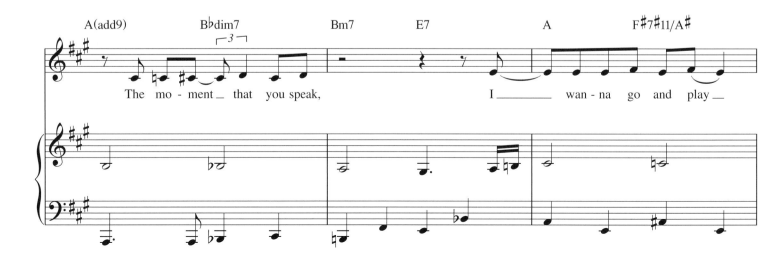

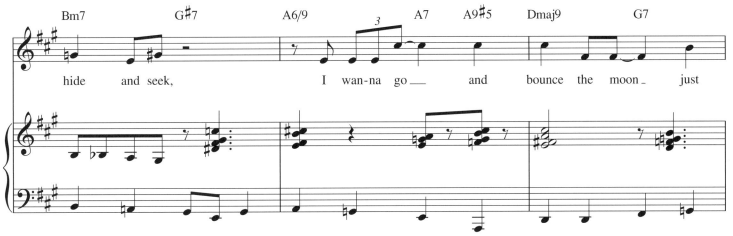

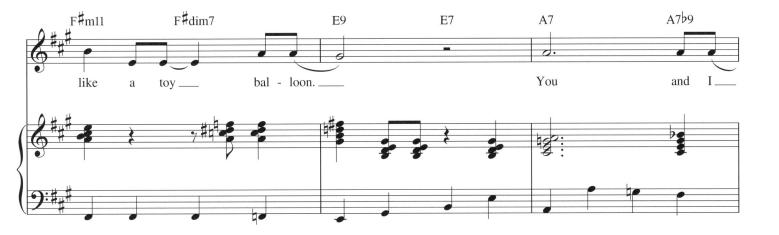

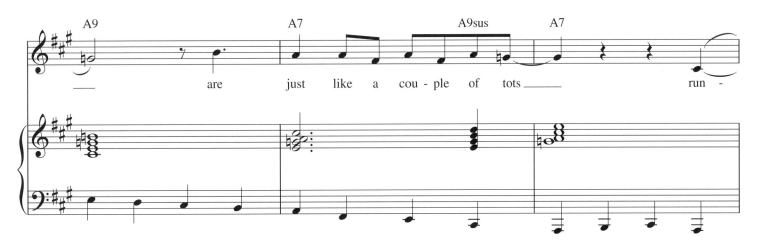

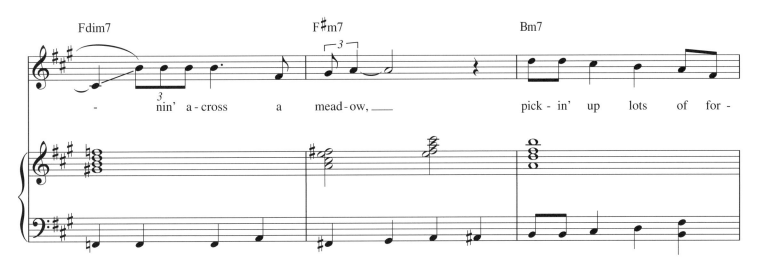

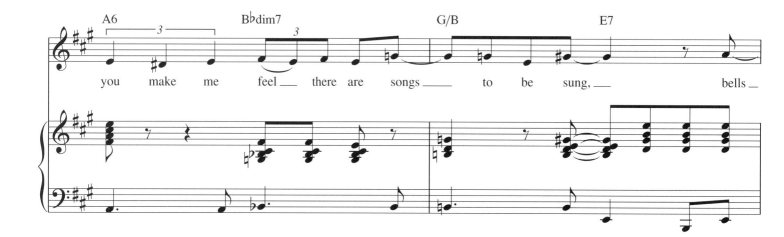

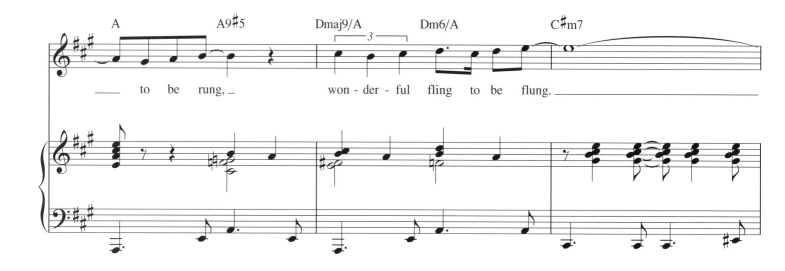

to - day, 'cause you, you make me

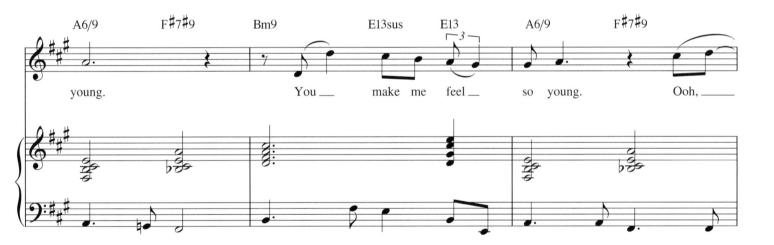

feel ___ so ___ young. You make me feel ___ so

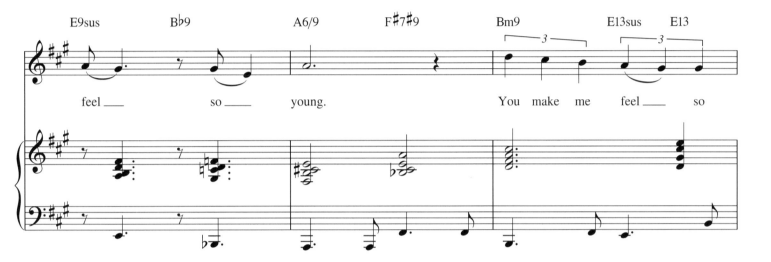

young. You ___ make me feel ___ so young. Ooh, _____

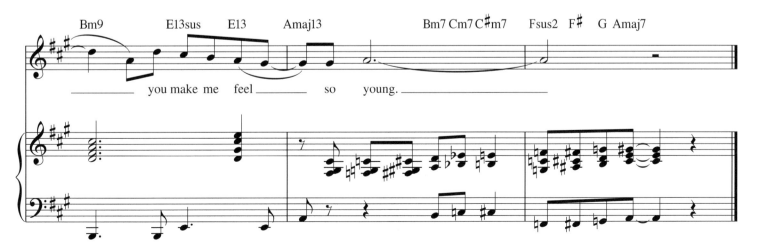

_____ you make me feel _____ so young. _____

YES SIR, THAT'S MY BABY

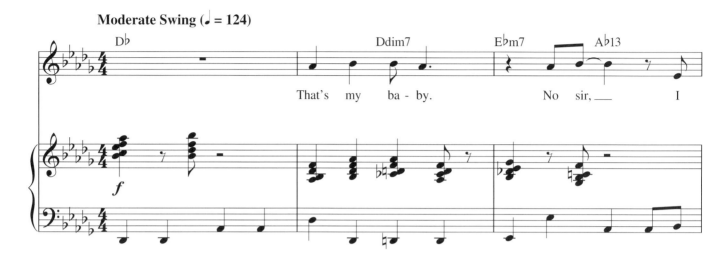

Lyrics by GUS KAHN
Music by WALTER DONALDSON

Moderate Swing ($\quarternote$ = 124)

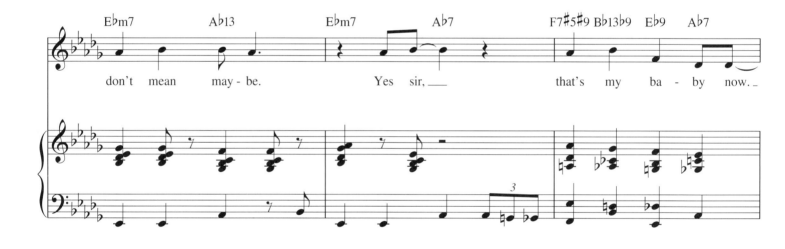

Copyright © 1925 (Renewed) by Donaldson Publishing Co. and Gilbert Keyes Music Co.
Gus Kahn's Canadian Rights Controlled by Bourne Co.
International Copyright Secured All Rights Reserved

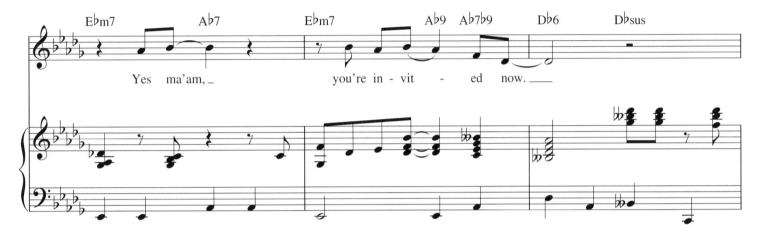

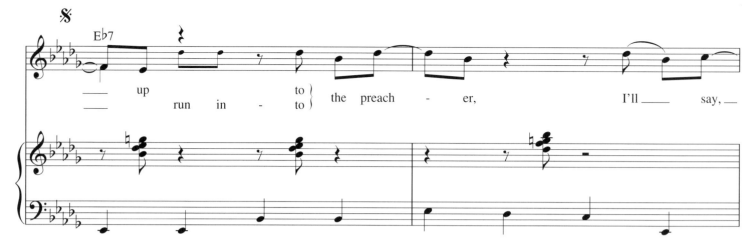

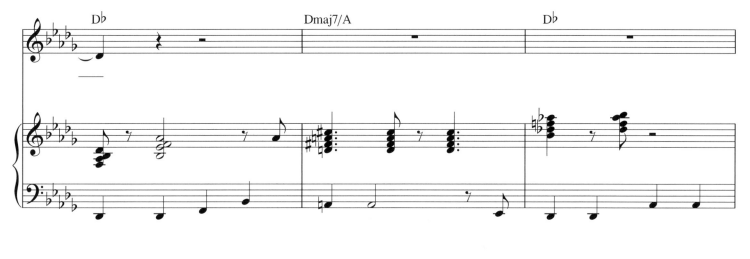

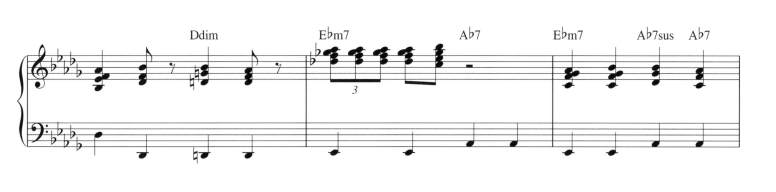

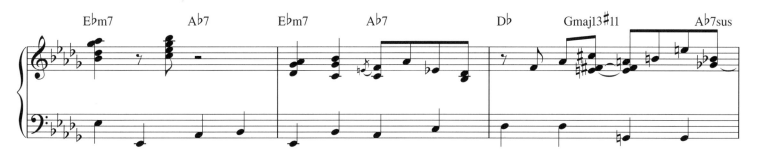

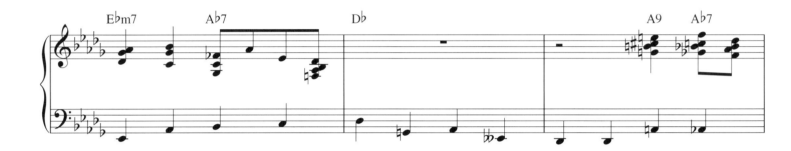

By _____ the way, ___ by _____ the

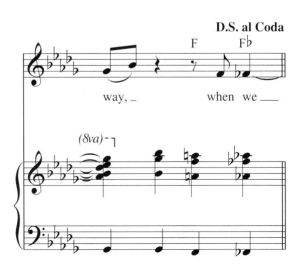

way, ___ when we ___